NEW POLITICAL ECONOMY

Edited by

Richard McIntyre
University of Rhode Island

A ROUTLEDGE SERIES

New Political Economy

Richard McIntyre, *General Editor*

Everyday Economic Practices

The "Hidden Transcripts" of Egyptian Voices

Savvina A. Chowdhury

Routledge
Taylor & Francis Group

NEW YORK AND LONDON

Routledge
Taylor & Francis Group
711 Third Avenue,
New York, NY 10017

Routledge
Taylor & Francis Group
2 Park Square, Milton Park,
Abingdon, Oxfordshire OX14 4RN

First issued in paperback 2015

Routledge is an imprint of the Taylor and Francis Group, an informa business

© 2007 by Taylor & Francis Group, LLC

ISBN 13: 978-0-415-54275-3 (pbk)
ISBN 13: 978-0-415-95552-2 (hbk)

Library of Congress Cataloging-in-Publication Data

Chowdhury, Savvina A.
    Everyday economic practices : the "hidden transcripts" of Egyptian voices / Savvina A. Chowdhury.
        p. cm. -- (New political economy)
    Includes bibliographical references and index.
    ISBN-13: 978-0-415-95552-2 (alk. paper)
    1. Egypt--Economic conditions. 2. Egypt--Economic policy. 3. Community development--Egypt. 4. Rotating credit associations--Egypt. 5. Informal sector (Economics)--Egypt. I. Title.

HC830.C47 2006
330.962--dc22   2006028473

Visit the Taylor & Francis Web site at
http://www.taylorandfrancis.com

and the Routledge Web site at
http://www.routledge-ny.com

For Jigar Jahan and Shahida

Contents

List of Tables

List of Figures

Acknowledgments

This book owes much to the guidance of Stephen Cullenberg, Gary Dymski and Keith Griffin. I would also like to thank Ric McIntyre for his detailed and helpful comments. My parents Ishrat and Azim have been incredibly selfless in all that they have done for me over the years. I am grateful also to Mishi for being my most loyal fan, and to Amy, who gave me the chance to return to Egypt in 1999. Last but not least, I am grateful to Sayad for his patience, understanding and sacrifice.

Introduction

Two Objectives

> *We refuse to see authenticity through a backward look that glorifies the past and rejects renewal. Not every thing in the past is glorious for it has some elements of backwardness. On the other hand, we refuse to distort our national character in the name of material or behavioral imitation of other societies. (Anwar el-Sadat, The October Paper, 1973).*

> *It will be our contention that transnational or neocolonial capitalism, like colonialist capitalism before it, continues to produce sites of contradiction, that are the effects of its always uneven expansion but that cannot be subsumed by the logic of commodification itself (Lowe and Lloyd, 1997, p. 2).*

Can economic development be re-conceptualized as a transformative process that need not replicate the trajectory of advanced industrialized countries? Is there a discursive space where we can engage local communities as they struggle to assert their notions of progress, development and economic justice? Are there notions of progress that do not necessarily entail adopting the path to "Modernity" as experienced by the Western world? These were the questions simmering at the back of my mind as I learned to negotiate the contradictions of doing participatory development planning in the repressed political climate of Egypt in 1999–2000. Throughout my time in Egypt and in my day-to-day interaction with Cairenes, I was constantly reminded of Akhil Gupta's observations on "other ways of being modern."

"Modernity" Gupta argues, is a story that the West narrates about itself. In this story the West is the protagonist, the "model, the prototype and the measure of social progress" (Stuart Hall, 1992, p. 313). Based on the European historical experience of the French and American Revolutions and inspired by the philosophical tradition of Liberal Humanism, the grand or *metanarrative* of Modernity promises individual freedom and social and political equality through the institution of representational government.

A subplot of the metanarrative of modernity is that of economic development. Like modernity, development too makes emancipatory prom-ises: eradicate poverty and disease, overcome hunger, empower women and bring all societies up to the standard of living enjoyed by the advanced industrialized countries. Both modernity and development propagate teleo-logical narratives: progress, according to this story of Modernity, occurs along a single path—the path taken by the advanced industrializes coun-tries of the West. For the formerly colonized societies of the Third World, to become "modern" is to attain notions of progress, civilization and ratio-nality as defined by the West (Gupta, 1997, p. 36). This involves adopting Westernized institutions (such as private property rights) that support the liberal democratic nation-state, and the increasing extension of the (undem-ocratic) economic practices of capitalism.[1]

Through the narrative of economic development, the historical experi-ence of capitalist industrialism in some countries is portrayed as an inevitable and universal trajectory for the rest of the world. The West in this narrative represents the "developed," and, conversely, "To be underdeveloped is to be a national community that is inferior, backward, subordinate, deficient in capital and resources, an inadequate member of the international order, and (by extension) a shabby imitation of the 'developed'" (Gupta, 1998, p. 40). Moreover, modernity-as-progress stands opposed to "tradition" as embod-ied in non- cultural, economic and political practices.[2]

This view of what constitutes progress is, Gupta notes, "an ines-capable feature of everyday life" (ibid, p. 37) in much of the developing world. And yet, he notes with reference to communities in Northern India, "it does not mean that people in rural India lead, or aspire to lead "West-ern" lives" (ibid). Gupta's observation applies equally to Cairene soci-ety—significant sections of which are increasingly returning to cultural, political and economic practices that are markedly *non-modern*. To the consternation of its proponents, instead of witnessing the unquestioned triumph of Western Modernity, the 21st century continues to experience the "irruption of non-modern cultural forms into the modern state" (Lowe and Lloyd, 1997, p. 5). In Egypt, resistance to the processes of modernity (such as those of individualization and secularization) has manifested itself in growing popular support for the Muslim Brotherhood (the Islamist political party that, though long banned, today constitutes Egypt's most powerful opposition party) the increasing adoption of the *hijab* by many "modern" Cairene women, as well as recurring acts of violence against Western tourists.

The contradictions that constitute Egyptian modernity as a lived real-ity are better understood in light of the critiques of Modernity as a unilinear, ethnocentric and homogenizing project. For theorists of *post*modernity, the grand, emancipatory metanarratives of Modernity are inherently contradic-tory. The work of Michel Foucault for instance, illustrates how Modernity gave rise to a set of repressive institutions and discourses which legitimized its mode of domination and control.[3] Indeed, much of the work of postmodern theorists such as Jean-Francois Lyotard, Jacques Derrida and Michel Fou-cault, examine the discursive practices through which "reason turned into its opposite and modernity's promises of liberation masked forms of oppres-sion and domination" ((Best and Kellner, 1991, p. 3). The grand narratives of emancipation, they argue, suppress the uneven experience of individual freedoms both within and outside the West. Within Western nations, while individual rights and liberties were to be enjoyed by all citizen-subjects of the modern nation-state, in practice this excluded indigenous peoples, women, slaves and those who did not own private property. Nor were these rights and liberties accorded to the peoples of the "non-West," whose narratives of independence were systematically suppressed by colonialist institutions.[4]

Similarly, Post-development theorists such as Jonathan Crush (1995), Arturo Escobar (1995; 1997) and Majid Rahnema argue that although the narrative of economic development promised the Third World the bene-fits of modern Western societies, development policies in reality often led to increased poverty, inequality, foreign indebtedness and environmental degradation. In Egypt, for instance, the contradictions of modernity have: (i) fostered an autocratic, politically repressive regime—and *not* a liberal democratic nation-state, (ii) created urban neighborhoods where thousands of children grow up in and around the old tombs of Cairo's "dead cities" (Egypt's version of shanty-towns), and (iii) led to the development of an economy where the largest and most vibrant sector is the informal sector.

"What then," asks Gupta, "does it mean to say that there are other ways of being modern" (Gupta, 1997, p. 37)? *Is* the historical experience of capitalist economic growth in the advanced industrial societies a *universal* inevitability for all societies worldwide? Is it desired? Are their possibili-ties for the creation of alternatives? To what extent has the self-representa-tion of modernity suppressed non- narratives of "alternative modernities" (Arjun Appadurai, 1991)? More importantly, to what extent has this subla-tion of alternative narratives prevented indigenous articulations of what it means to progress? To quote Tariq Banuri:

. . . The project of modernization has been deleterious to the wel-fare of Third World populations not because of bad policy advice or

malicious intent of the advisers, nor because of the disregard of neoclassical wisdom, but rather because the project has constantly forced
indigenous people to divert their energies from the *positive* pursuit
of indigenously defined social change, to the *negative* goal of resisting cultural, political and economic domination by the West (Banuri,
1990, p. 66).

Thus, the Post-development contention with the narrative of development is not to do with how the West caused the underdevelopment of
the non-West, or how the West gained from the persisting underdevelopment of the non-West[5] but rather how the development narrative continues to propagate the self-representation of the West, *and thereby suppress
and sublate other, non-Western narratives of economy and society* (Gupta,
1997; Lowe and Lloyd, 1997). Through their critique of development as the
self-representation of the West, theorists of postmodernity create a discursive space where notions of modernity, progress and development may take
newly defined and heterogeneous forms. Their project is to deconstruct the
familiar concept of development as capitalist industrialization and growth
by revealing the fact that capitalist practices exist among a heterogeneity of
local economic practices. In conceptualizing the way that non-modern or
non-capitalist practices influence the course, shape and form of development, postmodern theorists create alternative notions of what constitutes
development and progress. To quote Gupta,

> Modernity may have been instituted as a global phenomenon through
> colonial capitalism, but it was, in the process, resisted, reinvented and
> reconfigured in different social and historical locations. To emphasize
> the multivalent genealogies of "modernity" is to emphasize that the
> non-Western is not just a residual trace of a vanishing tradition but a
> constitutive feature of modern life (Gupta, p. 9, 1998).

The search for "alternatives"—whether in the form of alternative
modernities, alternative histories or alternative ways of organizing economic activity by post-modern Marxists—is a rejection of what I see as
the homogenizing and exclusionary tendencies of Modernity, or in its latest incarnation, neoliberal globalization. My own approach to the project
of recovering alternatives can be situated within two different perspectives
in the "alternatives" literature. First, from the perspective of the postmodern Marxist literature, my project involves "de-centering" capitalism;
from a post-development perspective it involves recovering alternative
epistemologies.

FIRST OBJECTIVE: DE-CENTERING CAPITALISM

Following the postmodern Marxist tradition, my first objective in unearthing local economic activities is to show that it is a misrepresentation to characterize all that is economic as "capitalism." The imaginary equivalence between "capitalism" and "the economy" overlooks the fact that there are people who, either consciously or unconsciously, in their everyday activities, are involved in a variety of "non-capitalist" practices.[6] That is, much of the material basis for human existence involves physical labor that is not remunerated by wages and nor are the products of this labor sold as a commodity in exchange for money in markets.

For instance, Feminist Economists have pointed out that one of the largest sectors of so-called advanced capitalist nations is *non*-capitalist in nature (Benería and Roldan, 1987; Folbre, 1991; Hartmann, 1981 and Fraad, Resnick and Wolff, 1994). The goods and services produced in the household sector of the economy are not produced for exchange in the market place, but rather meals are cooked, beds are made, clothes are laundered and homes are cleaned for immediate consumption. Empirical studies that have tried to measure the non-commodity sector have found that it accounts for 30–50% of total output in both rich and poor countries (Ironmonger, 1996) and that the full-time homemaker in the US spends between 52 to 60 hours a week preparing meals, cleaning the house, doing laundry and so on (Vanek, 1980). Despite its significance in terms of the proportion of the labor force it employs, the number of labor hours involved, the (imputed) value of its output, as well as, the significance of its role in the daily and generational reproduction of human beings, the household sector remains mainly "outside" mainstream notions of the economy.

Similarly Gibson-Graham have argued that if we were to recognize the self-provisioning, the self-employed, the retired, gift giving, volunteer work, illegal activities, barter, consumer and producer cooperatives—the "multifarious ways in which all of us are engaged in producing, transacting and distributing values" then "less than half of the total product of the U.S. economy is produced under" capitalist conditions (Gibson-Graham (2000), see figure 1 "Diagram of a Diverse economy" below). Gibson-Graham use the metaphor of an iceberg to depict the ways in which capitalist activities are given a place of privilege in dominant representations of what is said to constitute the economy. In this metaphor, the visible tip of the iceberg represents capitalist economic activities: commodity output produced by wage labor in capitalist firms. Beneath the visible waterline however, are a multitude of non-capitalist economic activities:

much of the material basis for everyday human existence involves physical labor that is not remunerated by wages and products that are *not* sold as commodities in exchange for money in markets. Despite their significance however, non-capitalist activities are de-emphasized, devalued or invisible in dominant representations of what is said to constitute the economy. Why then are capitalist activities depicted as being the only viable economic forms? And, what are we occluding when we equate capitalism to the economy?

Gibson-Graham (1993) have a term for the hegemonic representation of all economic activities in terms of their relationship to capitalism. They call such a representation *capitalocentrism,* whereby capitalism is the "center," or central reference, and other non-capitalist economic formations are defined in terms of whether they "complement" capitalism (the household sector), are located "inside the container" of capitalism, or are nascent

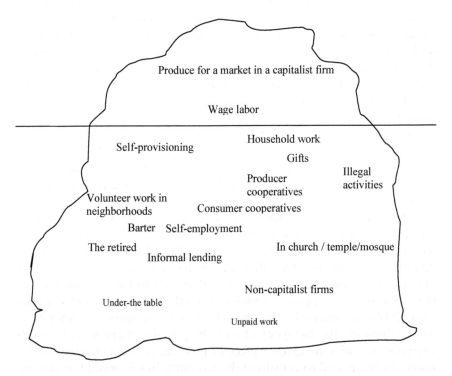

Figure 1. J.K. Gibson Graham's "The Economic Iceberg"

Source: J. K. Gibson-Graham (2006) *A Postcapitalist Politics*, University of Minnesota Press. Image drawn by Ken Byrne. Used with permission.

forms of capitalism (such as micro-enterprises in the informal sector). In their words, a discourse is capitalocentric "wherever noncapitalism is seen as either (a) the same as; (b) the opposite of; (c) the complement to; or (d) located inside capitalism itself" (Gibson-Graham, 1996).[7]

Capitalocentrism is particularly destructive for conceptualizing alternative paths to economic development. When the development discourse encounters other (non-capitalist) economic forms, the discourse of economic development depicts them as being "traditional," "pre-capitalist," "marginal," backwards, momentarily residual but unlikely to withstand the superior logic of efficiency and competition (Gibson-Graham and Ruccio, 2001). Thus, Gibson-Graham and Ruccio argue that the dominant narrative of economic development creates a totalizing discourse in which the Modern Western Capitalist Economy is presented as "the only viable and ultimately developmental form of economy" (ibid, p. x).

How can we produce an alternative representation of economic activity that recognizes the diversity of ways in which societies meet their material wants and needs? How can we theorize non-capitalist activities without seeing them as being traditional, marginal or nascent forms of capitalism? Can we tell the story of the Egyptian economy without telling it as the failure of Egypt to converge to the model of advanced industrialized capitalism? Are there anti-essentialist, anti-teleological stories of Egypt's economic development?

Using class analysis, post-Modern Marxists provide a *de-centered* conceptual framework for analyzing the heterogeneity of economic practices (Resnick and Wolff, 1987; Cullenberg and Chakrabarti, 2001, 2003). A de-centered approach to theorizing a *social totality* recognizes that any economic landscape consists of a heterogeneity of activities, based on context-specific customs and traditional ways of organizing labor and distributing the proceeds from an activity.[8] Moreover, at any given point in time, the political, cultural and economic practices that constitute a society are in flux—some types of activities are ceasing to exist, while others are coming into existence.[9]

Thus one of the most important implications of class analysis for my purposes is that in the postmodern Marxist view of a social totality noncapitalist activities exist side by side with capitalist activities. Furthermore, postmodern Marxists contend, there is no inner logic to the evolution of an economic landscape that propels it naturally and inexorably towards a preponderance of capitalist activities, and "to develop" does not necessarily mean to take some predetermined path from being a "backward" agrarian society to a "modern" capitalist industrial one.[10]

SECOND OBJECTIVE: RECOVERING ALTERNATIVE EPISTEMOLOGIES

How do I propose to theorize localized resistance to neoliberalism? What conceptual framework do I have? How do I theorize the asymmetrical (and often violent) encounters between local communities and supporters of neoliberalism? My second objective in unearthing local economic practices is to take an epistemological approach to theorizing resistance. Chapter Two argues that the policies that form the basis for neoliberal globalization are based on a specific epistemology of what constitutes economic knowledge. This same epistemology lies at the heart of "Western Science," which calls for an understanding of the world based on generalizable laws that can be applied universally, irrespective of context.[11] By contrast, local knowledge is bound by the particulars of culture, religion, geography and history (Apfell-Marglin ,1990; Guha, 1989; Gupta, 1997; Howitt, 2002). For instance, Western ways of knowing separate the private sphere of religious rituals from the public spheres of workplace institutions such as clinics and hospitals. In developing countries such as India however, work is infused with sacred rituals (Marglin, 1990), and holistic healing processes rely on the mind-body connection that comes with spirituality (Apffel-Marglin, 1990). Similarly, the Native American Nations movements, Australian aboriginal rights movements, the Maori in New Zealand, and indeed numerous indigenous movements worldwide, have challenged the ontological categories underlying neoliberal policies, arguing that they are based on an epistemological position that separates the economy from other social spheres such as the environment, tradition and culture.[12]

In the developing world, economic practices are infused with traditions, culture and spirituality and are often characterized by a contradictory co-existence—the traditional within the modern, the indigenous within the foreign, the private household within the public and the non-capitalist within the capitalist. Unearthing these contradictions destabilizes Western epistemology as well as the neoliberal assumption that economic laws are universally applicable, and that policies can be formulated in one context and then successfully applied to others.

Within mainstream economics, however, these contradictions that contest the neoliberal worldview are often seen to be part of the cultural sphere (or simply swept under the carpet as exogenously given preferences). Cultural space is discursively and epistemologically separated from the economy, for fear that the scientific knowledge of the economy will be contaminated by the non-scientific knowledge(s) of culture. And yet the cultural sphere has been the seedbed for much of the resistance to the homogenizing strictures of global capitalism. "Culture," Lowe and Lloyd remark, "obtains a political force when cultural formation comes into contradiction with economic or political logics that try to refunction it for exploitation or domination" (Lowe and Lloyd, 1997, p. 1).

In the United States, resistance to the exclusionary tendencies of capitalism in the late 20th century has been galvanized around what has been referred to as the narratives of "identity politics"[13] of new social movements. These new social movements have redefined the terrain where exclusion and domination take place. Political slogans such as "Gay and Proud," "Black is Beautiful!" and "Women unite, take back the night!" reveal the recognition that power and domination are constituted not just through physically coercive totalitarian states, but also through socially constructed categories of gender, race and sexuality. By challenging the very ontological categories through which meaning is constructed, these new social movements have brought to light the fact that the ideological struggles around race and gender in the United States are inextricably linked to the *material* conditions of minorities and women.[14] Similarly, the gay-lesbian-bisexual movement of the 1990s raised awareness of the *material* consequences of hetero-normativity. Thus, social identities such as religion, gender, ethnicity, and sexuality–supposedly located outside the sphere of the economy—have proved to be powerful sources of the desire to articulate alternative visions of social justice. These movements, Bowles and Gintis point out,

> . . . do not so much reject the importance of control over resources and distributive justice as they do deny the separability of economic moral and cultural outcomes, and assert the primacy of moral and cultural ends and the general status of economic concerns as means. These new political actors have supplemented the politics of *getting* with the politics of *becoming* (Bowles and Gintis, p. 10, 1986).

What is increasingly apparent is that social movements in other parts of the world share this refusal to separate the economy and economic justice from other social spheres such as culture and politics. Resistance to Western Modernity and the exclusionary tactics of capitalist activities is about both a struggle to assert context-specific notions of identity and a struggle for economic resources.

In those instances of rupture where local voices—such as the Chipko movement in India, or the uprising in the Chiapas, as well as environmentalist-, gay-lesbian-bisexual-, peace- movements in the industrialized nations—have broken into the discourse of economic development, they have done so by linking context-specific ideologies, histories, traditions with demands for economic justice. Embodied in the everyday forms of resistance of identity-based collective communities are the "hidden transcripts"[15] of culturally specific notions of progress, development and economic justice. Unearthing these hidden transcripts therefore, allows me to open up the discourse of economic development to re-conceptualize social change as an undefined, open-ended, heterogeneous transformative process. These quiet, daily struggles, I suggest, are manifestations of local communities struggling to assert themselves, their identities, their ways of organizing economic activity against the homogenizing and often exclusionary ways of capitalist economic development. In other words, in those instances where local voices have asserted themselves, both in the developing and industrialized countries, we catch a glimpse of alternative ways of knowing. I suggest that the normative content of these other epistemological frameworks provide us with alternative ways to conceptualize the economy and economic justice as defined by something other than the logic of commodification, efficiency and competition.

To return to the questions I raised at the beginning of this section, how do I propose to theorize resistance to neoliberalism? What conceptual framework do I have? I turn to postmodern Marxism, a narrative that is mindful of the fact that local economic practices are infused with culture, politics and history. The strength of this framework therefore lies in its rejection of economic essentialism and its underlying social constructivist epistemology. In a "class analytic" framework, economic activity is no longer emptied of all historical, cultural and ideological content: no longer does production and distribution take place in "a separate and rarefied social location" (Gibson-Graham, Resnick and Wolff, p. 1) as it does in dominant (neoclassical) representations of the economy. Nor is the economic sphere given more explanatory powers than the spheres of culture, politics or history in terms of understanding social phenomena. That is, unlike classical Marxist theories of resistance to capitalism, postmodern Marxists suggest that within the current restructuring of global capitalism, class antagonism between proletariats and capitalists are no longer the exclusive sites of contradiction. Rather, they are cognizant of the fact that resistance today is often constituted within discourses of culture and organized along the axes of ethnicity, gender, religion, sexuality etc:[16]

> . . . the analytical tasks facing Marxism are no longer confined to a rediscovery and deepening of the patterns of accumulation internal to "capital." They must rather reach beyond this topic, to a discovery and critique of the violence of everyday life that, in a continuous restaging of a logic of primitive accumulation, would forcefully construct (culturally

and politically as well as economically) identities and discourses in ways functional to varied patterns of capital accumulation: For example, how are racialized or gendered identities interwoven with the discourse of economic efficiency? How are communities, both geographical/spatial communities and communities of identities and needs, constructed and deconstructed by a discourse of culture of economic rationality, and how do they in turn give concrete forms to it? How are survival and identity struggles marginalized and subordinated, even silenced by the hierarchy of economic efficiency? The search for answers to questions such as these should lead Marxism to identify and valorize sources of resistance to capitalism . . . in the forms of identities that afford individuals and communities a degree of autonomy and avenues of escape from the strictures of social homogeneity (capitalist hegemony) but that are constantly under the threat of extinction (Callari and Ruccio, 1996, p. 7).

While restoring the forcefulness of culture as a source of resistance to the strictures of capitalism, postmodern Marxists nevertheless remain loyal to Marx's concern for the "materiality" of being.

THEORIZING EXCLUSION: WHY EGYPT?

Egypt is a clear instance of why it is imperative for the development discourse to create a discursive space in which to engage local communities. Egypt is the most populous nation in the Arab world with a population of about 76 million people. Young people at or below the age of fifteen comprise a third of the population. Participation in the modernist projects of nationalism and state-led industrialization however, has been limited. A succession of repressive regimes since 1952 has restricted participation in the process of economic development to a *quid pro quo* arrangement of economic entitlements in return for political acquiescence. As political and economic power has become gradually concentrated into the hands of an elite segment of the population however, resistance to the exclusionary tactics of the State has mounted.

Resistance has taken increasingly overt forms despite the omnipresent threat of brutal repercussions: from the relatively new grassroots democratic movement such as *"Kifaya"* (Arabic for "enough," the group is also known as the Egyptian Movement for Change), to the persistent popularity of a range of Islamist groups, from the mosque movement[17] to the more extremist Muslim Brotherhood. In 2005, the long-banned Brotherhood won 20% of the parliamentary seats. While acts of violence against Western tourists by the extremists attract worldwide headlines, still other quiet acts of resistance to the exclusionary nature of development has manifested itself in the mundane activities of a burgeoning informal sector that continues to elude regulation, enumeration and in general control and co-optation by the State.

One common aspect shared by both the strength and persistence of everyday informal institutions as well as extremist groups is their insistence on defining notions of participation, progress and development *on their own terms*. A second common aspect shared by the informal sector and the Islamic revivalist movements in Egypt is that they both depend on a collective identity: a *sha'abi* identity (meaning "of the common people") in the case of the institutions that support the economic transactions of the informal sector; an Islamic identity in the case of revivalist movements. The two identities are not mutually exclusive however: an Islamic worldview permeates the identity constituting processes of the *sha'ab*, and the *sha'abi* quarters are very often the strongholds of the Muslim Brotherhood. Resisting the consumerism, individualism and secularization associated with the modernization process, *sha'abi* neighborhoods in Cairo, hold on to a non-Westernized, collective identity to effectively organize and contest state policies that have for decades redistributed power and wealth to a Westernized elite. In other words, resistance to exclusion and the demands for voice and participation in Egypt combine both an interest in furthering the material struggles of everyday life with ideological identity-constituting process. More specifically, it is the identity-constituting processes of being Arab, or Muslim or *sha'abi* (or all of the above) that are proving to be the seedbed of organizing resistance to Western Modernity.

These alternative narratives of (non-) modernity however, exist in opposition to the ubiquitous dominant representations of Western Modernity. Tariq Banuri (1990) argues that while instability and conflict in developing nations is often interpreted as preventing economic development and the modernization process, political resistance to the state could alternatively be interpreted as "resistance to the rationalization and impersonalization of social existence entailed in the drive towards the formation of a Western-style state" (p. 51). *To what extent does the sublation of these non-narratives lead to their irrupting in a more violent form had they not had to contend with the totalizing discourses of Modernity and development?* How do the twin discourses of Modernity and Development engage these alternative narratives of non-modernity and development? Do they engage them? Is there a discursive space where we can engage local communities as they struggle to assert their notions of progress, development and economic justice? Can we conceptualize alternative, *participatory* paths to economic development? These were the underlying questions that formed the foundations of my fieldwork with United Nations Development Programme in Egypt (UNDP).

In 1999, the United Nation's Development Programme was involved in incorporating the elements of participatory research into the State's new physical plans for the tourist destination of Luxor in Upper Egypt. Though the UNDP's efforts were aimed at attempting to remedy the egregious exclusion of Luxor's communities from the planning process, I felt at the time that the "access-to-labor-markets" strategy of participatory development was an ambiguous invitation. It was in effect an invitation to participate in a hierarchical and inherently exclusionary process that, in its most overt manifestation in Luxor, takes the form of luxurious gated tourist resorts barricaded from the poverty of the surrounding community. During the course of my fieldwork with Luxor's communities I realized that the very term "participation" was in itself problematic. Participatory development, in the sense that it is used within the dominant discourses of economics, is limited to asking local communities to ratify a system of exclusionary practices. Chapter One therefore begins by examining this problematic.

The development literature of the late 1990s bears witness to the revival of interest in notions of participation, an empowered civil society, transparency in governance and the metaphor of "voice." Notions of voice, democracy and participation are crucial for unearthing the significance of local economic practices. Chapter One reviews these ideas within the development literature, distinguishing between three separate notions of participation: political participation in civil society, economic participation and participatory research. I argue that "participation" as it is most frequently used in the development literature is based on Liberal notions of individualism, and agency is confined by the public/private dichotomy. There are however, alternative notions of participation. I will argue in favor of a *labor theory of participation,* an idea present in the work of development economists such as Albert Hirschman (1970) and that constitutes the focal point for postmodern Marxist theory.

Chapter Two provides the epistemological foundations of the third notion of participation—that of participatory research and economic development. Participatory approaches to development and the postmodern Marxist labor theory of participation share common epistemological grounds. I suggest that both these approaches to participation lend themselves to a policymaking process that takes local customs and knowledge-based systems into consideration.

Chapter Three reviews the standard analyses of the Egyptian economy. After three decades of "opening" to capital, technology and markets, a recurring theme in the literature is Egypt's failure to experience capitalist industrial growth and development. Recurring questions vary along the lines of: "Why hasn't private sector investment been forthcoming in Egypt? Why haven't multinational companies been investing in Egypt despite government concessions since 1974? Why haven't 15 years of market reforms in agriculture brought about the large scale, mechanized "modern" (capitalist) farming with high yields and high value crops for exporting? Why hasn't the Egyptian economy experienced the agrarian transformation, urbanization, proletarization that are characteristic of advanced industrialized countries?" Is it possible to tell a story of the Egyptian development experience without telling it as the failure to converge to a model of capitalism?

Chapter Four is a case study of the dialectic between development planning policies, the narratives used to legitimize these policies and the hidden transcripts that have contested these policies in Luxor. Through the discussion of this dialectic I argue that Luxor and its surrounding areas have been the site of intensely fought struggles—both material and discursive. The dominant representation of the area is that of its role in the "economic progress" of the Egyptian nation-state. In this familiar narrative the region is represented as an engine of economic growth because of its ability to attract foreign capital through the global tourism industry.

Deconstructing this familiar narrative reveals that the viability of capitalist activity as an engine of growth is contingent on numerous overdetermined conditions of existence. The State has been creating these conditions through various processes such as institutional processes that foster separate "capitalist enclaves" that have special jurisdiction rights. The state is also attempting to promote capitalist activities in agriculture through new tenancy laws that have effectively led to a concentration of landholdings to promote larger mechanized farms. Lastly, through its control over the national media, the Egyptian State has been engaged in representational struggles: by appealing to the unifying forces of Egyptian nationalism over parochialism, it has been discursively dismantling the local communities' centuries-old customary rights to the monuments in the area.

Physically excluded from tourism enclaves, increasingly vulnerable to landlessness and periodically subject to attempts of eviction, the local communities have contested the State's plans for developing Luxor as an open-air museum. Their persistence in refusing to leave their fields, palm trees, houses and tombs constitute everyday acts of resistance against the exclusionary nature of the dominant narrative of economic development. By refusing to give up their rights to the area's tombs and temples, they are forcing the State and the tourism industry to share the revenue generated by Luxor's ancient cultural heritage. These sites of resistance therefore are the manifestations of the offstage discourse of localized, historically based forms of persistent levels of human deprivation, high rates of unemployment, revitalized democratic movements as well as entrenched religious extremism in Egypt suggest that participatory approaches to economic development have never been more necessary. But how is participation to be conceptualized? What kinds of ideas of participation are circulating the discursive space of economic development? The fifth and last chapter looks to local community-based models of participatory savings practices in Egypt.

Chapter One
Problematizing Participation

Participatory practice now seems capable of anything from raising social consciousness to increasing gender sensitivity and from resolving contradiction between growth and equity to getting relevant data for project design. The word "participatory has become the leitmotif of the day, almost banal in its broad applicability. This is the moment to reappraise the idea after its transformation from rogue idea to standard practice and to see it afresh for what it is, what it isn't, what is profound and what, after all, is still subversive about it. (Freedman, 1997, page 769)

The capitalist economy, then, produces people; and the people it produces are far from ideally equipped with democratic sentiments and capacities (Bowles and Gintis, 1987, page 135).

DEVELOPMENT: HOMOGENOUS OUTCOMES OR A HETEROGENEOUS PROCESS?

Proponents of neoliberal economic policies have three main concerns. First, they stress the role of markets in allocating resources and advocate minimal government intervention. Second, they emphasize the role of private property as an institution that promotes the "good" incentives that lead to investment and economic growth. Third, they advocate a particular notion of what constitutes "sound" fiscal and monetary policy: those that balance the government's budget and keep inflation low. These then constitute the main *outcomes* desired by neoliberal regimes: low inflation rates, balanced-budgets, liberalized domestic and international markets and the privatization of an economy's resources. In the 1980s and 1990s, the ability of

17

developing countries to restructure their debt, obtain development loans
and foreign aid from the Bretton Woods institutions were conditional upon
their striving for and achieving these outcomes.[1]

The Neoliberal agenda and its institutional proponents (such as the
World Bank and the International Monetary Fund) have been criticized by
economists such as Ravi Kanbur, Dani Rodrik, Amartya Sen and Joseph
Stiglitz[2] for its view of development as a set of *homogenous outcomes*.
Contrary to the view of development as a set of homogenous outcomes,
the latter have instead argued in favor of conceptualizing development as a
heterogeneous process.

Stiglitz for instance, argues that proponents of neoliberalism overlook
the fact that *outcomes* such as high standards of living could be achieved
through repressive regimes and oppressive working conditions or conversely, through a participatory civil society and high levels of worker participation in the industrialization process.[3] Development, he argues, is not
(as it was previously thought) primarily a "technical" problem of how best
to allocate resources through "better planning algorithms, better trade and
pricing policies, better macroeconomic frameworks" (Stiglitz, 1998, page
4). Instead, he suggests development should be seen as a *transformative
process* (ibid, page 23). Similarly Rodrik (2003) points out that there are
many—and not only one—ways to develop, pointing out that even among
capitalist industrialized nations American-style capitalism differs greatly
from Swedish- and Japanese-style capitalism. Moreover, he points out, even
within the relatively similar European welfare states, diverse institutional
arrangements govern labor and markets.[4]

The *2000/2001 World Development Report: Attacking Poverty*,
attests to the fact that even within the program cycles of the World Bank,
poverty alleviation strategies have shifted from being focused on outcomes
such as the accumulation of physical capital to more process oriented
approaches that have emphasized governance, institutions, and "promoting
opportunity, facilitating empowerment and enhancing security" in 2000
(page 6). Written under the guidance of Ravi Kanbur,[5] the Report draws
heavily on "*Voices of the Poor: Can Anyone Hear Us?*"[6], and is organized
around the notion that policies must address the "voicelessness and power-
lessness" articulated by poor people in *participatory* poverty studies (WDR,
2000/2001, page 15) that deprive them of their "human capabilities."

Amartya Sen's seminal work on "human capabilities" (1981, 1985a,
1985b) as well as his work with Jean Drèze, *India: Development and Participation* (1996) and his more recent work on *Development as Freedom* (1999)
has played a pivotal role in theorizing development as a process. Sen argues
that while outcomes such as long, healthy lives, low mortality rates, and

high standards of living are uncontested development goals, there may be more than one process through which these ends are brought about: There is a distinction between "culmination outcomes" (that is only final outcomes without taking any note of the process of getting there, including the exercise of freedom) and "comprehensive outcomes" (taking note of the processes through which the culmination outcomes come about) (Sen, 1999, page 17).

PARTICIPATION AS ACCESS TO MARKETS AND SOCIAL CAPITAL

Drèze and Sen (2002) distinguish between two concepts of participation: *political participation* and *economic participation*. Political participation refers to the ideal that "democratic participation requires the sharing and symmetry of basic political rights—to vote, to propagate and to criticize" (Drèze and Sen, 2002, page 9). This form of "elementary and fundamental" participation however is more effective "if there is some equity in the sharing of economic resources as well" (ibid). *Economic participation* therefore refers to the sharing of society's material wealth. Both types of participation, they point out, are "intimately connected with demands for equality" and hence social change (ibid). Lack of equality in one can affect outcomes in the other: "economic inequality can seriously compromise the quality of democracy, for example, through the influence on the electoral process, on public decision-making, and on the content of the media" (ibid, page 9). Neoliberal discourses on development however, tend to conflate these two distinct notions of participation and, when they do discuss economic participation, they emphasize outcomes over processes.

The most typical approach to addressing economic participation in the mainstream development literature involves promoting people's access to markets. Are poor people benefiting from market reforms? If not, then what are the barriers to their participating in the various markets and hence partaking in the benefits of economic growth? For instance, the World Development Report acknowledges that

> Even when markets function, they do not always serve poor people as well as they could. Physical access to markets can be difficult for poor people living in remote areas. Regulatory barriers often stifle economic activity in sectors where poor people are likely to seek jobs. And access to some markets, especially for financial services, can be difficult for poor people since they often engage in small transactions, which traditional market participants find unprofitable or insignificant (*The World Development Report*, 2000/2001, page 64).

In other words, the discourse of mainstream development economics accedes that while markets may create economic opportunities, not all members of society have access to these opportunities. The success of the East Asian countries, for instance, was due in large part to the fact that public policies in these countries promoted widespread access to market opportunities. State-led investment policies promoted high levels of literacy, provided basic health care and instituted relatively egalitarian land reforms to allow people to participate in markets (Sen, 1999). To promote economic participation therefore, mainstream development policies advocate improving people's access to markets.

One popular policy to promote the participation of those who are socially marginalized and typically excluded from the benefits of market reform—especially, poor, women-headed households—is to facilitate their access to credit. Microfinance institutions patterned along the line of the Grameen Bank now command broad support among international donor agencies.[7] The argument for creating financial institutions to service the poor is based on the fact that although low-income households have little in the way of (formal) collateral, fixed monthly salaries or even credit histories, they nonetheless possess significant amounts of "social capital." The success of the Grameen Bank in Bangladesh for instance, has been attributed to the high levels of "social capital" that serves to screen, monitor and enforce the proper use and repayment of small-scale loan among low-income communities. Microfinance institutions rely on a community's level of social capital to deal with principal-agent problems by having local communities screen, monitor and enforce loan repayment.[8]

The significance of social capital in this context is viewed in terms of what it contributes to outcomes such as economic growth. Influenced by works such as Putnam's *Making Democracy Work* (1993), the underlying argument is that economic productivity is higher in communities where people participate actively in associations (be they local government associations, voting groups or soccer associations as in Putnam's study of Milan, Italy) than in communities where there are fewer social arrangements for people to voice their concerns and participate in activities that promote their collective well-being. In other words, one of the many factors necessary for economic growth are energetic local organizations where individuals can feasibly activate a social network. Consequently, the project design documents of international donor agencies (such as the World Bank) now routinely call for fostering "social capital" and an active associational life as a way to increase the participation of civil society in development projects.

The word "capital" in "social capital" imparts the sense that social networks, or "good" cultural values such as a work ethic or frugal consumption habits that lead to a high propensity to save, are valued because they are a necessary input in the production process and hence economic growth.[9] This notion of participation, in other words, clearly serves the "efficiency" goals of an international financial institution such as the World Bank. Promoting economic participation therefore, is in effect reduced to promoting outcomes such as "high repayment rates" on micro-loans, the number of new "start-ups" and ultimately economic growth.[10] This outcomes-centered notion of economic participation as "exclusion from markets" does not address the open-ended possibilities of "participation as process."

Appraising "good" cultural values such as work and savings ethics or the ability to maintain social networks by the extent to which they contribute to economic productivity is tantamount to evaluating human capabilities in terms of the magnitude and significance of their contribution to gross national output. This view of social capital is reductivist: it reduces participation in collective associational life to what it contributes to economic output. The institutions that make up "social capital"—social networks and cultural norms that lead to high levels of trust and reciprocity among individuals in a society—serve more purposes than lowering the transaction cost of economic activity. They also serve as the foundation for the various forms of associational lives that in turn form the basis through which communities participate in the political and economic spheres. "The bettering of human life does not have to be justified by showing that a person with a better life is also a better producer" (Drèze and Sen, 2002, page 7). As Sen points out with respect to human capital, social capital defined in terms of civic participation as well as cultural norms of trust, cooperation and reciprocity, is not *just the means to an end but ends in themselves.*

Nancy Folbre in *The Invisible Heart: Economics and Family Values* (2001) argues that the "capital" metaphor in "social capital" is misleading if what economists are trying to measure are reciprocity, trust and cooperation. "Trust can be accumulated and sometimes we draw on funds of goodwill. But not everything can be bought and sold, or stored for an indefinite period of time. Trust and goodwill are not easily transferable from one person or one country to another" (ibid, page 77). She goes on to note that, "Something about the way individuals work together usually makes a group more (or less) than the sum of its parts. Love and trust ensure a kind of reciprocity that usually elicits more effective cooperation than would any formal agreement" (2001, page 75). Furthermore, she argues, "Social capital is seldom defined as to include feelings or emotions. Yet it is feelings and concern for others—developed through contact and interaction with them—that provide crucial reinforcement for trust and cooperation" (page 77).

To the contrary, in fact, the drive towards Modernity and capitalist economic development often involve societal changes that de-emphasize concern for others by fostering the values of competition and individualism at the expense of cooperation at the community level and collective well-being. Developing countries tend to have high levels of community and kin-based social capital that are often undermined during the process of market liberalization:[11]

> . . . in the process of development, this organizational and social capital is often destroyed. The transformation may weaken traditional and authority relationships, and new patterns of migration may sever community ties. The problem is that this process of destruction may occur before new organizational and social capital is created, leaving the society bereft of the necessary institutional structure with which to function well (Stiglitz, 1998, page 15).

The neoliberal emphasis on liberalizing markets therefore, has led to a limited notion of economic participation. For Sen, the issue of concern is not markets *per se*: "To be generically against markets would be almost as odd as being generically against conversation between people" (ibid, page 6). Rather, the issue that is often at the heart of participatory development is, do men and women have the "substantive freedoms" that enable them to enjoy "the kind of life he or she has reason to value" (ibid, page 87)? For Sen, the neoliberal preoccupation with outcomes such as liberalized markets, has led to "the neglect of the central value of freedom itself" (Sen, 1999, page 28).

Bowles and Gintis on the other hand, contend that the ethics of the marketplace are inimical to substantive notions of participation. In *Democracy and Capitalism: Property, Community, and the Contradiction of Modern Social Thought* (1987), the authors argue that the undue emphasis on markets not only leads to the neglect of freedom, but actually works to "erode a democratic culture" (Bowles and Gintis, 1987, page 128). The ability to boycott a particular market for instance, is not equivalent to participating in the decision-making process that may change outcomes in that market through the exercise of one's "voice." Withdrawing from a market is in effect tantamount to "voting with your feet" (or wallet), and in Albert Hirschman's schema, constitutes an "exit" strategy.[12] This tendency to prefer exit over voice as a strategy promotes a notion of participation at the individual over group level, thereby undermining the proclivities of communities to collectively organize and fight for their substantive freedoms. Bowles and Gintis argue that by promoting exit over voice strategies, markets have in effect depoliticized community-based participatory action: "The person who feels strongly about street crime or air pollution can either organize to improve the social and physical environment, or they can 'shop' for a community with a more desirable bundle of characteristics" (Bowles and Gintis, 1987, page 135).[13] By promoting exit over voice, they note, markets may actually discourage participation in the types of collective action that bring about change in a community: "The extensive reliance upon markets thus undermines the conditions conducive to a high level of participation and a vibrant democratic culture" (Bowles and Gintis, 1987, page 135)

MARKETS, CAPITALISM AND DEMOCRACY: A FUNDAMENTAL CONTRADICTION

Indeed, for Bowles and Gintis, the problem inheres not merely in markets promoting individualistic behavior over collective action, but is embodied within the principles that underlie the institution of Liberalism's nation-state. They argue that at the heart of the nation-state lies a fundamental contradiction. While liberal philosophy promotes social equality through the extension of *personal* rights, capitalism promotes economic inequality through the sanctioning of *private property* rights. The contradiction therefore lies in the discourse of "rights": on the one hand, liberalism promises the expansion of personal rights, on the other hand the "the expansionary logic of capitalist production" (Bowles and Gintis, 1987, page 29) relies on a hierarchical and undemocratic way of organizing economic activity, that excludes people from having a voice in the "substantive decisions that affect their lives" (ibid, page 66). Under capitalism, owners of firms are able to take actions that substantially affect the lives of workers: they are able to organize the production sphere to suit the interests of capital over workers, they are able to exercise power over a community's investment decisions, and they are able to exert power over the state thereby limiting the extent of democratic control over economic activity (ibid, page 67). This predominance of property rights over personal rights means "no capitalist society may be called democratic" (Bowles and Gintis, 1987, page 3).[14]

The contradictory claims of private property rights over personal rights led to institutional arrangements in Europe and North America that initially limited suffrage and political participation to those who possessed land and wealth and to those who were formally educated. Those who did not own property, as was often the case with women, had few civil rights, and in the case of slaves, no civil rights. These restrictions were justified on the basis that only those who had "real stakes" in society should be allowed to have a say in the affairs of the nation (Bowles and Gintis, 1987, page 42). Over time, with the extension of universal suffrage and the expansion

of expansion of civil liberties, representative government and the discourse
of liberalism appeared to curb the glaring excesses of capitalist tendencies,
while concurrently obscuring "the underlying privilege and domination" of
property-based rights.

The historical legacy of this exclusion is that within liberal democratic
nation states today, individual rights are experienced unevenly: political
participation continues to favor those who own wealth and property and
disfavor certain ethnicities and women.[15] Sen documents the compromised
quality of democracy in the United States where historical exclusions continue to have ramifications for minorities and their ability to participate in
the US economy even today. "For example, the extraordinary deprivations
in health care, education and social environment of African Americans in the
United States help to make their mortality rates exceptionally high, and this
is evidently not prevented by the working of American Democracy"(Sen,
1999, page 155). Thus, he points out, a participatory political system such
as a liberal democratic nation-state, does not necessarily guarantee citizens
a voice in the economic realities that form the material basis for their lives.

By calling for the establishment of institutions that support markets,
neoliberal policies explicitly propagate the view that to grow, develop and
modernize, Third World countries must adopt political institutions that
are similar to (if not patterned directly after) those that exist in western
Europe and the United States. Drawing on the work of New Institutional-
ists such as North (1991) and Williamson (1997), as well publications such
as the *World Development Report* (2002), "Building Institutions for Market," recent incarnations of neoliberal policy recommendations, have called
for defining and enforcing private property rights as a necessary condition
for successful capitalist economic growth. These policies create a global
framework to foster the expansion of capitalist multinational corporations
worldwide and propagate undemocratic ways of organizing economic activity under the guise of development. Indeed, the success of outcomes such as
trade liberalization and free capital mobility are contingent on Third World
nations adopting Western-style institutions such as private property rights
and dismantling indigenous notions of property rights and social justice.
Moreover, by defining economic participation in terms of people's ability to
access or exit from global markets, neoliberal policies promote a restricted
notion of participation (as already discussed above).

If development is a *transformative process*, asks Stiglitz, then how
should a country proceed, "transformation to what kind of society and for
what ends?"(Stiglitz, 1998, page 23). And if developing countries are to
adopt institutions patterned after those of Europe and the United States,
what forms of participatory—or exclusionary—arrangements will they

inherit? For example, the World Bank's notions of participatory civil society clearly favor certain forms of civil society in Egypt over others. Development projects sponsored by the Bank and the Government of Egypt have excluded the participation of a large number of anti-western, Islamic NGOs (both militant and non-militant). In a politically repressed landscape such as that of Egypt's where associational life (not to mention democratic rights) is formally curtailed by Law Number 32 of 1964, "civil society" in effect refers in actuality to *government sanctioned* Non-Government Organizations. "Empowering civil society" in the context of urban Cairo has been restricted to empowering the state-backed Federation of Egyptian Industries—a consortium of relatively wealthy businessmen that is able maintain a NGO status. International donor institutions such as the World Bank and the United Nations turn to these state-sanctioned organizations, which in effect become the vehicles through which donor agencies fund, monitor and evaluate their development projects. The agendas of these state-sanctioned organizations have proved to be significantly different than the agendas of community-based Islamist movements, some of which are clearly anti-Modern. Though the Egyptian state has frequently suppressed the more militant Islamic fundamentalist groups (such as the Muslim Brotherhood), it has been unable however, to squelch the mosque-based Islamic revivalist movements that have gained political momentum by articulating Islamic concepts of collective identity and social justice.

In the dominant neoliberal narrative of what constitutes participation there is little discursive space in which to engage the significant sections of Egyptian civil society that are clearly opposed to aspects of Liberalism and the nation-state. Despite the renewed interest in participatory development and the rhetoric of voice and empowerment, the concept of participation as it is most frequently used in the development literature is problematic. Is there a discursive space where we can engage these local communities as they struggle to assert their notions of progress, development and economic justice? Can we conceptualize alternative, participatory paths to economic development? Not, it would appear, when we rely on concepts that remain within a western, modernist, capitalocentric discourse of progress and development. The remaining sections of this chapter therefore, turn to heterodox economic theories to conceptualize participatory development as an open-ended and heterogeneous process.

LABOR THEORIES OF PARTICIPATION

In order to address Bowles and Gintis' point that "no capitalist society may be called democratic," any attempt to conceptualize development as a participatory process must account for democratic ways of organizing not just the politics, but also the economy. If economic participation refers to sharing of society's material wealth, how are the fruits of the development process shared among the members of a society? If within capitalist organizations, owners of firms are able to take actions that substantially affect the lives of workers, then what types of economic activities allow workers to have a voice in the organization of the workplace? Under what conditions can workers have a say in the industrialization process of an economy? To what extent do they have a say in how the material gains from development are distributed? Approaches to conceptualizing development based on the democratization of the economy add a further aspect to the discussion on economic participation. I refer to these approaches as "labor theories of participation." The first part of this section provides a brief discussion of the participatory role of labor in the workplace and in the industrialization process as a whole as presented in the heterodox literature. The second part of this section will address a postmodern Marxist "labor theory of participation" to deepen our understanding of participating in the economy. Postmodern theory provides a third perspective on participation—that of participatory knowledge, in the last part of this chapter.

a) Participatory Processes, labor and the metaphor of "voice"

In a keynote address to the Industrial Relations Research Association, entitled *Democratic Development as the Fruits of Labor*, Joseph Stiglitz (then Senior Vice President and Chief Economist at the World Bank Group) outlines what is tantamount to a "labor theory of development." In it he argues that the labor movement in the advanced industrialized countries has played a crucial role in the development process. Unions, he contends, have contributed to economic development through mitigating income inequalities, stabilizing industrial relations, contributing to firm-specific knowledge, setting workplace health and safety standards, child labor standards and so on.[16]

He stresses the fact that the labor market is subject to dynamics that are very different than the markets for other factors of production—dynamics that, he argues, neoclassical economics, and in particular, the Arrow-Debreu model of general equilibrium overlooks. The starting premise for his labor theory of development is that "Labor is not like other factors. Workers have to be motivated to perform" (Stiglitz, page 4). The central issue in labor economics, he contends, is how to design an appropriate mix of incentives so that on the one hand, workers do not shirk and on the other, firms can minimize their monitoring costs. Because of this asymmetry in terms of firms not knowing if workers are putting sufficient effort into their jobs, the labor market is characterized by imperfect information. Imperfect information arising from this "principal-agent" problem leads to a breakdown of the Fundamental Theorems of Welfare Economics (since perfect information is an assumption of the Arrow-Debreu general equilibrium model). In the labor market therefore, a competitive equilibrium is not Pareto optimal, and "issues of efficiency cannot be separated from issues of distribution" (Shapiro and Stiglitz, 1984).

Principal-agent problems also arise in the labor market from the perspective of workers and their stake in corporate governance. Asymmetric information plays a role in the conflicting interests of workers, managers and shareholders in terms of how firms are run. He illustrates this point by analyzing the East Asian crisis from workers' viewpoint. The risky borrowing undertaken by firms in East Asia preceding the crisis may have benefited international creditors and promised shareholders a high rate of return, but it also exposed the firm to the soaring interest rates, falling exchange rates and declining aggregate demand when the crisis unfolded. The question that Stiglitz raises is, would the firm have undertaken these loans if workers had been part of the management process?

> Had workers had a significant voice in management, they would have strongly argued against the firm taking such a position, unless the firm provided adequate job security (severance benefits) to the workers. As it was, the workers had no say. . . . In this case, there was a natural alliance between international creditors and equity owners (supported by one of the financial institutions, whose officials, in trying to ward off such a default, spoke repeatedly of the sanctity of such contracts, paying little heed to bankruptcy being a core part of capitalism, and the at least *implicit* contract between workers and their firms that were being torn up, all in the name of protecting creditor rights (Stiglitz, 2000, page, 10).

Because labor markets are characterized by asymmetric information in various forms, historically, context-specific institutional forms have arisen to maintain worker morale and productivity. Using Hirschman's (1970) analytics of voice and exit, as well as Aoki's (1994) work on low and high worker involvement in the workplace, Stiglitz compares and contrasts two alternative "stylized" paths to industrialization. The "high road" to market-based industrialization involved long-term relationships between creditors, firms and their customers that are stylized as being based on "Voice," commitment and trust. Stiglitz contrasts this to the "low road" where relationships between creditors, firms and their customers are "arms-length, market-oriented and competitive."

Societies that developed by taking the "high road" to growth, he argues, experienced the industrialization process differently than those that have taken the "low road" to development. The "high road" to development involved relatively stable, long-term contractual relations between firms and workers, between firms and their creditors and between firms and their customers. Labor market experiences in high road societies were marked by long periods of secure employment, with compensation that often included profit sharing as well as wages. Firms often paid for training costs, viewing it as long-term human capital investment. They avoided Principal-Agent problems by inducing high effort, morale and productivity through worker involvement in shop-floor decision-making. Dissatisfaction in this system was addressed through "voice" processes as opposed to the "exit" mechanism (Hirschman, 1970). Workers addressed their grievances through collective bargaining procedures. Group solidarity and cohesiveness was maintained through low wage differentials across society.

By contrast, the "low road" economies were characterized by higher levels of unemployment and "efficiency wages"—higher than market wages paid by firms to discourage labor turnover. Dismissal was used as a credible threat in these societies to discipline workers and job security was low. In contrast to "high road" societies, workers in "low road" societies were more likely to pay for their own training to increase their marketability. Wages were contractual and the existence of large differentials provided incentive for emphasizing individual achievement over group solidarity.

This relationship between firms and workers was intricately connected to capital markets. Firms that took the "high road" enjoyed long-term relationships with their creditors. Institutionalized relationships based on trust and loyalty between firms and creditors meant that loans were made and investment was undertaken on a longer-term basis, allowing firms to reap the returns to the human capital invested in workers. The debt-to-equity ratios for these firms were higher than that of "low-road" firms. Firms in low-road firms had to have lower debt-to-equity ratios to provide flexibility in the face of their vulnerability to vicissitudes of the market. Their arms-length, market-oriented relationship with creditors meant that their loans were of a shorter-term horizon than those of firms in "high-road" systems. Consequently low-road systems experienced higher labor turnover, longer recessions with higher levels of unemployment and under-investment in firm-specific capital.

Stiglitz argues that East Asian firms became prone to crises when they adopted an "unwise" mixture of the two (incompatible) systems: short-term borrowing from arms-length creditors (low-road institution) while still carrying high debt-to-equity ratios (a feature of high road systems). He worries that

> . . . one of the more adverse consequences of the East Asian crisis may be the abandonment of the "high road" as firms are being encouraged to break long standing implicit contracts with workers, to "downsize" in response to new economic realities—even if downsizing implies forcing long term workers into unemployment (page 15).

Thus, Stiglitz' arguments for participatory processes in development are grounded in his work on market failures in the labor and credit markets. His notion of participatory development emphasizes the notion of worker participation both at the shop floor level as well as in the overall industrialization process of an economy. The neoliberal, outcomes-centered approach to development, he argues, overlooks the fact that societal transformation could be achieved through repressive regimes and oppressive working conditions or conversely, through a participatory civil society and high levels of worker participation in the industrialization process.

b) Postmodern Marxism and Class as a Participatory Process

While the preceding approach to re-conceptualizing development as a heterogeneous process has been fruitful in terms of thinking about the role of labor in the course of industrialization, Postmodern Marxists argue that they do not go far enough in terms of theorizing the normative concern for exclusion and distributive justice. For the purposes of re-conceptualizing development as a participatory and heterogeneous process, the strengths of postmodern Marxist theory lie in two areas. First, it provides a conceptual framework for analyzing the heterogeneity of economic practices through class analysis.[17] In doing so, it provides an alternative rationale for theorizing economic justice around the notion of surplus labor and exclusion. Second, class analysis addresses the fact that the struggle for economic justice has been organized around "identity politics," embedding economic agents and practices within their historical, contextual, and cultural specificities. The following sections elaborate on the relevance of these areas for conceptualizing development as a participatory process.

Class as Process, Exclusion and Distributive Justice

The first reason why class analysis is crucial for re-conceptualizing development as a heterogeneous process is that it provides a conceptual framework for analyzing the heterogeneity of economic practices based around the normative concern of exclusion and surplus labor. In doing so, the "class analytics" framework, allows for a process-oriented notion of participatory development.

When the mainstream development literature addresses economic participation, it does so from the perspective of participation in markets (as have I have argued in the section titled "Participation as access to markets and social capital"). In this view of participation, the emphasis is on the equality of outcomes—that everyone should have the opportunity to participate in (or exit from) markets—and, that participation in local and global markets is important to bring about capitalist economic growth. However, capitalist activities are undemocratic and hierarchical: a worker who participates in a capitalist enterprise has the ability to enter into a contract with an employer, but has no voice in the decisions affecting the organization of the production process or the distribution of its profits.

By contrast, the Postmodern Marxist view of participatory development is a process-oriented notion of participation. The Postmodern Marxist answer to the question "How are the fruits of the development process shared among the members of a society?" would be to say, "That depends on the extent to which the workers in a society have the ability to appropriate, control and distribute the surplus value that they produce." In other words, a Postmodern Marxist conceptualization of participatory development involves participation in, not just the generation of social wealth, but also in the decisions concerning who will appropriate this wealth and how it will be distributed. This way of looking at how any economic activity is organized makes visible the extent to which workers have a voice in the substantive decisions that affect their lives.

The Postmodern Marxist concept of participation rests on Marx's critical distinction between necessary and surplus labor. Necessary labor is the number of hours workers needs to work to maintain their subsistence level or, "produce the consumables customarily required by the producer to keep working"(Resnick and Wolff, 1987, page 20). The remaining hours of work performed by the worker beyond this necessary labor is surplus labor. Postmodern Marxists are careful to point out that the demarcation between surplus and necessary labor is not a fixed, but a movable boundary: "What is necessary/surplus is not predetermined in some humanist or cultural essentialist sense, but is established at the moment of appropriation itself" (Gibson-Graham, Resnick and Wolff, 2000).

From this distinction between necessary and surplus labor arises an embodied, context-specific concept of participation. Recognizing that workers produce a surplus product over and above the needs of their subsistence gives rise to the question "What happens to this surplus?" Who participates in the performance of "surplus labor"? Who appropriates it and who distributes it? Who is excluded from the appropriation of "surplus labor"? This embodied notion of participation, organized as it is around labor practices, is therefore a "labor theory of participation." Marx points out that under certain ways of organizing economic activity—such as capitalism—workers are deprived of the fruits of their own labor and excluded from participating in the decision-making processes concerning the appropriation and distribution of this surplus labor. He identifies this exclusion as *exploitation*.

Unlike other conceptualizations of class based on gradations of income or power, the Postmodern Marxist concept of class involves evaluating the extent to which workers participate in the performance, appropriation and distribution of *surplus labor*. Marx contrasts the production, appropriation and distribution of surplus under capitalism with that under primitive communist, slave, ancient, communal or communist. When the physical product of surplus labor (or the monetary value of it) is appropriated by someone other than the direct producer of this surplus labor the worker is said to be in an exploitative relation with the appropriator of surplus value.

Using this distinction between necessary and surplus labor, any given economic practice can be categorized according to the extent to which those who produce surplus labor participate in its appropriation and distribution. Table 1.1 below depicts this "disaggregated class nature of society" (Cullenberg and Chakrabarti, 2001, page 171). The independent class process (class sets 1–4), involves a single worker performing and appropriating his/her own surplus. These activities describe a self-employed person who sells her commodity in the market and may (class set 1) or may not (class set 3) pay herself a wage. The independent class process may also describe an individual who lives by himself and appropriates the surplus labor from his own cooking and cleaning etc. Hence his output takes non-commodity form and his remuneration is in non-wage form (class set 4).

The capitalist class process involves practices whereby each worker in a capitalist enterprise produces in a day enough wealth to sustain her- or himself (for which he or she is compensated in the form of wage) and also a surplus, which is appropriated by the individual capitalist or by the board of directors of the capitalist firm. If the output is sold in a market then this activity describes class set 5; if the output is supplied to a firm further down a vertically integrated production process (taking therefore noncommodity form) then this activity describes class set 6. Since the physical product of surplus labor (or surplus *value*—the monetary value of it) is appropriated by someone other than the person who produced it, under these two class sets, the worker is said to be in an *exploitative* relation with the appropriator of surplus value.

Table 1.1. The Class Diversity of Economic Activities

Class Sets	Class Process	Example	Workers Access to Surplus Labor	Worker Remuneration	Output Distribution
1	Independent	A self-employed person who pays him/herself a wage and sells her product in the market	All	Wage	Commodity
2	Independent	All	Wage	Noncommodity	
3	Independent	A self-employed person who does not pay him/herself a wage and sells her product in the market	All	Nonwage	Commodity
4	Independent	A single-person household	All	Nonwage	Non-commodity
5	Private or State capitalist	A capitalist or state-capitalist firm that employs waged labor and sell their commodities in the market.	None	Wage	Commodity
6	Private or State capitalist	A capitalist or state-capitalist firm supplies its commodity to another firm further along down a vertically integrated production chain.	None	Wage	Noncommodity

(continued)

Table 1.1. The Class Diversity of Economic Activities (continued)

7	Feudal or slave	A commodity producing plantation that uses slave labor	None	Nonwage	Commodity
8	Feudal or slave	A plantation that uses slave labor but does not sell its product in the market	None	Nonwage	Noncommodity
9	Communal	Consistent with some form of worker-owned firm or worker cooperative	Shared	Wage	Commodity
10	Communal—	Consistent with "public goods" or with the state provision of education and health care	Shared	Wage	Noncommodity
11	Communal	Shared		Nonwage	Commodity
12	Communal	Communal households as described by Fraad, Resnick and Wolff	Shared	Nonwage	Noncommodity

It is important to note that capitalist class processes may be *private* or *state* capitalist class processes. A private capitalist class process can be exemplified by a corporation where a board of directors appropriates the surplus value of workers. Under state capitalism, one or more state officials appropriate the surplus labor and distribute it. Extensively developed by Resnick and Wolff (2002) in *Class theory and History: Capitalism and Communism in the U.S.S.R.*, this distinction between private and state capitalist practices is especially relevant in the context of Egypt, where key industries were nationalized by Gamal Abdel Nasser under the nomenclature of "Arab Socialism." However, as Resnick and Wolff show, "a communist class structure is then one in which the producers and appropriators are the same people, whereas the class difference of capitalism is precisely that the appropriators are different people from the producers" (ibid, page xi). Nationalized Egyptian industries where a board of state functionaries appropriates the surplus labor created by workers who are excluded from the appropriative moment, therefore constitute a capitalist, and not a communist, class process.

The communal class process involves workers collectively performing, appropriating and distributing their surplus labor. "Democratic labor-based" firms such as the Mondragon cooperatives in Spain are examples of a communal class process describe by class 9. Workers are members of the businesses in which they work and participate in the appropriation and distribution of surplus labor on the basis of "one person, one vote." Class set 10 is consistent with the state provision of services such as health and education where workers are paid wages and participate in the appropriation and distribution of surplus labor. Under these state-organized economic activities output is distributed in non-commodity form. Class sets 11 and 12 describe households where all members participate in the performance or surplus labor and share in its appropriation and distribution. If the output is sold in a market as it might be on a communal family-farm, then it takes the form of class set 11.

Last but not least, it should be noted that exploitation also occurs under feudal or slave class processes (class sets 7 and 8). The producer of surplus on the medieval European manor often delivered his/her surplus labor (or its products) directly to the lord of the manor. Ties of tradition, religion, fealty, loyalty and force ensured that the serf delivered the surplus to the feudal lord. Fraad, Resnick and Wolff (1994) argue that the traditional patriarchal household resembles a feudal class process. The various forms of sharecropping that exist in the Third world today also constitute feudal class processes.

Thus, under the language of class the economic terrain emerges as constitutive of heterogeneity of internally differentiated social and economic practices. Capitalism is recast as merely one among many forms of organizing production and capitalist institutions have to continually negotiate their existence among a diversity of non-capitalist practices, with differing ideologies and cultural constructions. If capitalism is conceptualized as one type of class process where surplus labor is performed by a worker but appropriated and distributed by the capitalist, then there are other types of class processes where surplus labor may be collectively or individually performed, and appropriation may occur at an individual or collective level. This form of analysis reveals that far from moving towards a monolithic, universalizing form, economies are fragmented, heterogeneous constituted by diverse practices that may be feudal, independent, capitalist, communal as well as other forms that remain to be conceptualized.[18]

Using the class analysis framework, postmodern Marxists have shown that these diverse economic practices involve different levels of worker participation and exclusion. Cullenberg (1992) in particular has argued in favor of work-place arrangements where all those who work at a site of production have equal rights to share in the appropriation of surplus labor. In these "democratic labor-based" firms such as the Mondragon cooperatives in Spain, workers are members of the businesses in which they work and participate in the appropriation and distribution of surplus labor through on the basis of "one person, one vote." He characterizes these firms as being consistent with collective surplus appropriation in terms of class processes bundled with the non-class processes (the conditions of existence) that allow for democratic decision-making. "The collective form of appropriation (or collective appropriation for short refers to the initial site of surplus labor production where all individuals employed at that site share equally (one person, one vote) in the appropriation of the surplus labor" (Cullenberg, 1992, page 23).

A labor theory of participation based on class analysis therefore theorizes an additional aspect of economic participation in the development process. It differs from other heterodox analyses of economic participation by bringing to the forefront the fact that depending on the way economic activity is organized, the performers of surplus labor may or may not be participants in the appropriation and distribution of surplus labor. Participation in the development process therefore, may involve not only workers' rights to participate in shop-floor decision-making, in collective bargaining for wages and working conditions, but also that democratic decision-making should be extended to the realm of distributive justice. This normative concern for exclusion allows a previously suppressed aspect of participation to enter the discourse on participatory development.

Class as Process: Exclusion and Identity

The second reason why class analysis is crucial for re-conceptualizing development as a participatory process is because of its ability to provide a theoretical framework to address the ontological challenge posed by local communities around the world and their everyday economic practices.

Mainstream economics' understanding of individual agency restricts its notions of participation to the ballot box or the market. As already argued however, not only is this an outcomes-centered, exit-based notion of participation, but it also downplays a more process-oriented, voice-based notion of participation. In this discourse, Bowles and Gintis point out that voice-based

participation is cast as being prohibitively costly and likely to be characterized by the "free-rider" problem. "It of course follows from this argument
that self-interested individuals will not engage in such life-threatening acts as
making revolution, fighting for democracy or engaging in civil disobedience
to secure civil rights" (Bowles and Gintis, 1987, page 137).

Contrary to this view however, recent events have brought to light
the increasingly unified resistance of seemingly disparate local communities
to the neoliberal worldview. Voices in the advanced industrialized nations
raised in demonstrations against the IMF and World Bank in Seattle, in
Genoa, in New York and other places, are often speaking the same language
as Maoris asserting indigenous rights to natural resources, the CHIPKO
movement's rights to India's forests and the *Adivasis* indigenous rights to
properties being claimed by the Indian government.

> Maybe the protests in Seattle and Washington look unfocused because
> they were not demonstrations of one movement at all but rather con-
> vergences of many smaller ones, each with its sights trained on a spe-
> cific multinational corporation (like Nike), a particular industry (like
> agribusiness) or a new trade initiative (like the Free Trade Area of the
> Americas). These smaller, targeted movements are clearly part of a
> common cause: They share a belief that the disparate problems with
> which they are wrestling all derive from global deregulation, *an agenda
> that is concentrating power and wealth into fewer and fewer hands.*
> Of course, there are disagreements—about the role of the nation-state,
> about whether capitalism is redeemable, about the speed with which
> change should occur. But within most of these miniature movements,
> there is an emerging consensus that building community-based deci-
> sion-making power—whether through unions, neighborhoods, farms,
> villages, anarchist collectives or aboriginal self-government—is essen-
> tial to countering the might of multinational corporations (Naomi
> Klein, 2000).

Furthermore, in those instances where local voices have asserted
themselves, both in the developing world and in the developed world,
they have done so by linking context-specific, ideological and cultural
considerations with demands for economic justice. That is, the social
identities such as religion, gender, ethnicity, sexuality—supposedly constituted
outside rarefied location of the economy—have proved to be the powerful
origins of the desire to resist the exclusionary process of Modernity and
capitalist economic development. In the Egyptian context for example, local
community-based movements have organized around a *sha'abi* identity in

the popular quarters of urban Cairo and an Islamic and pan-Arab identity in the case of the "Muslim Brotherhood."[19] Resisting the consumerism, individualism and secularization associated with the Western values adopted by the Egyptian elite for instance, *sha'abi* neighborhoods in Cairo, hold on to a non-Westernized identity to collectively organize and contest the exclusionary outcomes of neoliberal policies. Similarly in other parts of the world, where local communities have successfully organized collective resistance to Western Modernity and its adherents, they have done so by drawing on the identity-constituting processes of being *sha'abi* in Cairo, a Zapatista in the Chiapas, an *Adivasi* in India or a "tree-hugging environmentalist" in North America.

> These new movements do not so much reject the importance of control over resources and distributive justice as they do deny the separability of economic moral and cultural outcomes, and assert the primacy of moral and cultural ends and the general and the general status of economic concerns as means. These new political actors have supplemented the politics of *getting* with the politics of *becoming* (Bowles and Gintis, 1987, page 10).

Moreover, while protests such as the one in Seattle, or Argentina, or the uprising in Chiapas or the CHIPKO movement in India, command the public's attention through news headlines, still other daily instances of resistance remain below the radar of the world's media. These quiet, everyday economic practices, I argue, are manifestations of local communities asserting themselves against the exclusionary tendencies of capitalist economic growth and development.

Based on the assumption of exogenously given preferences, Neoclassical theory is unable to speak to these identity-affirming, localized community-driven resistance to Western Modernity and an outcomes-centered notion of development. Vice-versa, the strength of Postmodern Marxist theory lies in its ability to speak to the multitude of local movements, with their cultural particularities, historical contingencies, and epistemological "otherness." Whereas classical Marxism, was confined by its ability to theorize collective community-based participation in the economy to speaking of the proletariat, Postmodern Marxists distinguish themselves from classical Marxists by recognizing

> . . . The emergence of new political identities and subjects, such as the new social movements in both Western and non-Western societies; the failure of the (really existing) socialism; the collapse of the simple opposition between capitalism and (really existing) socialism that stood

> at the center of the cold war; the in-going reorganization of patterns
> of accumulation and attendant (national and global) changes in the
> division of labor and the distribution of wealth and resources (Callari
> and Ruccio, 1996, page 4)

That is, they acknowledge that the classical Marxist question of socialism
versus capitalism, long held as *the* problematic underlying social transformation and justice, does not speak to all the "varied struggles that occupy
the space of liberatory politics" (ibid, page 5). Rather, they recognize that
current resistance to neoliberalism is often activated by the fact that neoliberal emphasis on economic efficiency homogenizes, subordinates and mar-
ginalizes the "forms of identities that afford individuals and communities
a degree of autonomy and avenues of escape from the strictures of social
homogeneity (capitalist hegemony)" (ibid, page 8).[20]

Thus, "participation" as theorized by post-modern Marxists refers
to participation in a) the class processes of performing, appropriating and
distributing surplus value and b) the non-class processes of the social construction of identities along the lines of race, ethnicity, gender, religion etc.
The power of class analysis in conceptualizing participation and development therefore lies in its ability to theorize every economic practice as a site
that is overdetermined by context-specific processes of culture, religion and
the social construction of identities. By theorizing the ideological struggles
around the material conditions of human existence, class analysis "refuses
to ascribe priority and privilege to any social dimension" or "reduce an
event or being to a root cause" by honoring the specificity of every site,
practice and conjecture" (Gibson-Graham, Resnick & Wolff, 2001).

All this is possible due to the underlying social constructivist epistemology that rejects the scientific aspirations of economics knowledge and
takes knowledge to be a discursive construction. In this sense, the labor theory of participation embodied in class analysis overlaps the third and last
notion of participation in the literature—that of participatory research.

PARTICIPATORY RESEARCH

The third notion of participation that I raise in this chapter and then explore
further in the following chapter is that of *participatory research*—a look
at the concept of participation from an epistemologically conscious stance.
Here, it is important to bear in mind the distinction that Sen (1999) makes
between democratic *ideals, institutions* and *practice*. Democratic *ideals* refer
to ideals such as the freedom of expression, the public accountability of
leaders, the equitable distribution of power etc—the rhetoric that is often

espoused by states if not always put into practice. Democratic *institutions* refer to the vehicles through which the above ideals are practiced—such as, constitutional rights, effective rights, the electoral system, parliaments and assemblies, free and open media and so on. Ultimately however, whether or not democratic institutions are successful in expressing democratic ideals is dependent on the *practice* of democracy. The practice of democracy in turn, is contingent on a wide range of social conditions such as the level of education, social norms, political traditions, popular organizations—and, as put forth by post-development, post-modern and post colonial theorists, even in the process of knowledge-creation itself.

The position that knowledge is "interested" and not neutral, that the state of knowledge is contingent on the community that creates it and should therefore be a dialectical process among the members of a community and between different communities, is based on what is known as social constructivist epistemology. For social constructivists, meaning is "taken from context and conveyed by language"(Dow, 2001). They stress the discursive nature of knowledge. Knowledge, says Feyerabend (1988) "resides in the ways we speak"; it is constituted by a plethora of forms such as lists, stories, dramatic accounts, histories; it is contingent on time and space, and "rigor" can come from any systematically laid out argument—"good science is good conversation," as McCloskey puts it. Ultimately, social constructivists are epistemologically anti-essentialist: there cannot be one True way to know the world hence; to them reality is socially constructed and it is always already theory-laden.

Given the diversity of societies, the acknowledgement of such complexities has led many to reject a *social constructivist epistemology* and argue that such a stance leads to cultural relativism and hence critical paralysis. However, Postmodern theorists (and certain development practitioners as I will argue in the following pages) have argued that an overdetermined epistemological stance may be perceived as critically paralyzing only if the object of theory is to simplify complex social phenomena in the search for causal essences and "True" knowledge of the world. If on the other hand, the object of theory is to produce knowledge that is context-specific, then the methodology of knowledge creation should involve careful analysis of each situation, case by case. The overarching objective then becomes not to apply universal laws and principles based on standardized axioms, but to understand a particular phenomenon as being affected by various cultural, historical as well as economic processes.

> Overdetermination is a form of relativism to be sure, but that does not imply a quietude, whether scholarly or politically (if you want

to separate them out). It does imply, I think, an attention to case study and the specificity of each analysis as done by institutionalist economists and not the strategy of empirical work as is classically done with econometrics, which tries to separate distinct explanatory factors and weight or sign them (Cullenberg, 1999).

In the development literature, proponents of participatory research, notably Norman Uphoff (1988 and 1992) and Robert Chambers, have called for a dialectical policymaking process that involves a dialogue between policymakers and the objects of their policies. As such, this form of policymaking is likely to be reflective of a specific context, interested in voicing the situational particularities of a community and explicit about issues of distribution and power. Chapter Two discusses the rise of this concept from its radical origins in the pedagogy of Paolo Freire to its incorporation into the mainstream literature of the international development institutions. Despite the ease with which it has become part of project cycles of institutions such as the World Bank, I argue that participatory research is based on an epistemological stance that offers a radical break from the philosophical traditions of European Enlightenment.

CONCLUSION

My aim in this chapter has been to differentiate between three separate notions of participation in the development process. Political participation, as conceptualized by the individual rights and freedoms of the citizen-subject of the modern nation-state, is firmly grounded in the ideas of the European Enlightenment. The preeminence of private property rights over individual rights however, has circumscribed the political and economic participation of those who historically have been property-less. Promoting institutional arrangements such as private property as part of an unqualified set of policy recommendations for developing nations therefore may be problematic.

Closely tied to political participation is the concept of economic participation. By promoting a Western model of development and progress, mainstream development policies remain within the confines of a limited notion of participation in the economy. Economic participation within the dominant narrative is conceptualized as "access to markets." In this framework, notions of agency are once again circumscribed by the institution of private property and are limited to the ability to buy and sell goods (e.g. by micro-entrepreneurs), the ability to borrow in the credit market, or buy and sell labor in the labor market. A vibrant democratic culture requires a deeper understanding of the ways in which communities can have a *voice* in the decisions that affect their daily material existence. Postmodern Marxism offers a framework for theorizing a deeper and voice-centered notion of participation.

The third approach to participation is that of participatory research. I argue that the epistemological foundations of participatory research provide an intellectual rationale for reasserting the value of alternative experiences and ways of knowing. The following chapter therefore looks to epistemology to raise the following questions: Why has mainstream development theory traditionally ignored indigenous knowledge-based systems? Could it be that there is something about the nature of theory itself that is at issue here?

Chapter Two

Is Participatory Research Development's Postmodern Turn?

My aim in this chapter is to draw connections between postmodern theory and the participatory research work that I did as a consultant for the United Nations Development Programme in Egypt. During this period I was exposed to the possibility that development practitioners (by whom I mean community-based organizations, non-government organizations, multilateral agencies as well as state agencies) were practicing a form of economic development that was far removed from that of economic theorists. It seemed to me that while development policies at the macroeconomic level were based on a positivist[1] methodology of economics, development practitioners at the field level were operationalizing policy-making processes that allowed communities to create their own agendas and conduct their own research and analysis, taking indigenous customs and knowledge-based systems into consideration. I was struck by the connections between what they were doing and what is known as postmodern "ways of knowing."

The position that knowledge is "interested" and not neutral, that the state of knowledge is contingent on the community that creates it and should therefore be a dialectical process constitute currents of what is known as "postmodern" ways of knowing, or epistemology. Although postmodern ways of knowing have been making inroads into economics since the 1980s,[2] many have argued that postmodernist thinking leads to nihilism accompanied by critical and political paralysis (Portes and Kincaid, 1989; Sorj 1990). During the course of my fieldwork in Egypt however, I was intrigued to find that grassroots organizations were operationalizing a postmodernist epistemological stance that economic theorists are having difficulty incorporating into their models. Why, I was forced to consider, has mainstream development theory traditionally ignored local knowledge-based systems? Postmodern theorists have argued that economic theory's Popperian penchant for demarcating scientific from non-scientific knowledge gives no forum to knowledge-systems that are not based on the philosophical traditions of European Enlightenment. Could it be that there is something about the nature of theory itself that is at issue here? My arguments in this chapter therefore build up to the following question: Is the move towards participatory research in development economics a move towards a postmodern/ dialectical/discursive way of creating knowledge?

WHY POSTMODERNISM?

My underlying motivation is to find a theoretical space where it is possible to conceptualize economic development as something other than along the lines of industrialization and modernization as experienced by the West. This is the project of Postmodern Marxists (as well as Post-Colonial and Post-development theorists) who theorize the existence of non-capitalist (and non-modern forms) of society and economy, and recognize that there are alternative ways to develop. While there is an extensive literature on the currents of postmodernism in art, architecture, literary theory, philosophy and economics, following Cullenberg, Amariglio and Ruccio (2001), I wish to draw out four major currents in postmodern theory that are pertinent to the project of conceptualizing alternative, participatory paths to development.[3]

The first current views "postmodernity" as the latest phase of capitalism in world history: "the universal extension of a differentiated mode of production that relies on flexible accumulation and mixed production to incorporate all sectors of the global economy into its logic of commodification" (Lowe and Lloyd, 1997, p.1). The work of Frederic Jameson (1991) has been instrumental in disseminating the view that the capitalist logic of commodification has been homogenizing the social spaces of not just the economy, but also increasingly those of culture and politics. Jameson illustrates this point with reference to the work of neoclassical economist Gary Becker, who theorizes individual decision-making in spaces such as the family using the cost-benefit logic of the utility-maximizing rational economic agent, or homo economicus.

A second current in postmodern thought concerns the basic epistemic assumptions underlying the "grand narratives" that emerge out of the European Enlightenment. Jean-Francois Lyotard's *The Postmodern Condition: A Report on Knowledge* (1984) best exemplifies the radical ramifications of this second strand of postmodern thought. Through his "report" Lyotard casts suspicion on "humanist metanarratives" such as the Enlightenment philosophies of liberalism and Marxism, both of which have made radical promises of emancipatory societal change. Both narratives, Lyotard points out, make these emancipatory promises in the belief that scientific progress will bring an end to different forms of oppression.[4] On the other hand, both narratives have suppressed and sublated the oppositional voices of women, slaves, those who did not own property as well as conquered colonized peoples. Both narratives, notes Mcloskey, have used the "claim of transcendence as a stick to batter the opposition" (McCloskey, 2001, p.109). Similarly the narrative of 'Progress through Science' in development economics has made emancipatory promises but in effect failed to fulfill promises to eradicate hunger and poverty (Escobar, 1995). To the contrary, Lyotard points out, in the name of progress and emancipation, the metanarratives of modernity have delivered new forms of unfreedoms and destruction such as totalitarian states, ethnically motivated genocides, the atom bomb and environmental destruction.

Furthermore, Lyotard is suspicious of the all-knowing, purportedly universal subject of "humanist metanarratives." By making the claim that these metanarratives are based on a scientific methodology of creating knowledge, theories of modernity subscribe to the classical epistemological position that "True" knowledge of the world is possible. Truth is possible, because the "subject" of a theory (text or narrative) is ontologically separate and distinct from the object of study. This ontological separation allows the subject to examine the object of study in an unbiased, disinterested fashion. This, Cullenberg et al suggest, is a "misspecification of the nature of the subject" and one that postmodernists claim, has had grievous consequences:

> The problem of knowledge had been to specify how knowing subjects could apprehend a mostly dumb and intractable world of objects. But postmodernists have often written on the question of knowledge from the point of view that this problem is really a red herring. That is, postmodernists often claim that the problem of knowledge in classical epistemology is built upon a misspecification of the nature of the subject and ignores the impossibility of ever pulling apart the knower from the known (Cullenberg et al. p.20).

In other words, postmodernists are critical of the very ontology of classical epistemology: there cannot, they argue, be "a god's eye perspective" and metanarratives do not embody the "view from nowhere."[5] Instead, postmodernists espouse an epistemological position suggests that truth is stand-point based and contingent on one's subject position: "the unique experiences either of individuals or the groups to which they belong are today productive of 'situated knowledges' and "knowledge may be 'relative' to the diversity of cultures and sets of experiences" (Cullenberg et al. p.13). Thus, postmodernists question the idea that scientific knowledge can be created in a void, by neutral, unbiased subjects, rejecting the epistemological claim that theories can reflect "Truth." Rather, scientific knowledge is itself "something that is socially constructed, something that is created through acts of interpretation and by negotiation among members of a specific community" (Caldwell, 1982, p.xi).[6] The nature of the contemporary subject they argue, is not the unified, universal "Man" of modernity, but the fragmented, "de-centered" subject of identity-based knowledges (Cullenberg et al. p.12) of post-modernity. Consequently, postmodern theorists call for the emergence of a proliferation of voices based on multiple and varied subject positions.

A third category of postmodernism is a stylistic one that focuses on textual analysis. Just as Lyotard argues for "de-centering the subject," so Jacques Derrida argues for "de-centering the text." In *Of Grammatology* (1976) for instance, he argues in favor of de-centering texts through deconstruction-a method of textual analysis in which the multiple meanings of a text emerge through their relationship to other texts and to the reader's subject-position and interpretation. The practice of deconstruction elicits Derrida's argument that Western thought is logocentric, or based on "a center"-a Truth, an Essence, or God-from which all meaning is derived. Deconstructionism, Cullenberg et al. point out, dances in playful contrast to the "minimalism and parsimony thought to be characteristic of many 'high modernist' movements in culture and theory" (Cullenberg at al. page, 18). Given that the meaning(s) of texts is (are) unstable and open to multiple interpretations, then for postmodern theorists the act of creating knowledge "aspires to a civilized conversation among equals, what the German sociologist Jurgen Habermas calls the ideal speech situation and what the British political philosopher Michael Oakeshott called 'the conversation of mankind'" (McCloskey, p.107, 2001).

The fourth category though which to understand postmodernism is that of a strategy of critique: "attempting to create thought and action 'outside' of the perceived constraints of modernism (and here modernism ranges from modernization and economic development strategies in a post-colonial world to the 'high modernism' of formalist literature and mathematics)" (ibid, p.5). As a strategy of critique, postmodernism emphasizes textual deconstruction, bringing to light alternative stand-point based narratives, and sites of contestation where local practices resist the logic of commodification and the exclusionary and homogenizing tendencies of late capitalism. In this critical vein, a common objective of postmodern theorists is to call attention the fact that economic practices at the local level encompasses a diversity of practices that are molded by particular cultural constructions. Moreover, these practices are based on indigenous knowledge-creation processes that, while not following a scientific methodology, need to be valued on their own merit. Informed by a postmodernist suspicion of metanarratives such as "development through scientific progress" or liberation through (capitalist) representative democracy, the challenge for postmodern theorists is how to theorize these local, indigenous knowledge based understandings of economy and society without falling prey to using the ontological categories of western science.

Drawing on the works of Foucault (1980) and Said (1979), Arturo Escobar (1992, 1995, 1997) provides a textual analysis of the development discourse, as opposed to a systemic criticism of capitalist economic development.[7] Hence, his is a radically different position from that of those who have criticized the global capitalist economy as a system, in that it is an epistemological critique as opposed to a systemic one. Earlier critiques of development, while critical of the global capitalist economy as a system (Andre Gunder Frank (1966), and Paul Baran(1973), for example), were all based on theories that held the view that "current economic knowledge reflects the true state of a real entity called 'the economy' (generally understood as a locus of capitalist dominance)" (Gibson-Graham and Ruccio, 2001, p.162). This position makes it difficult to re-conceptualize development and "think outside the box," since the global capitalist economy is unquestioned as an "extra-discursive reality" (ibid, p.165). In other words, the reality of global capitalism is beyond the scope of discussion, it is, as Gibson-Graham and Ruccio put it, "disproportionately powerful by the virtue of its indisputable reality" (2001, p.165).

Why, asks Escobar (1995) has development been so resistant to radical critique? Why, to paraphrase him, is it apparently impossible to conceptualize alternatives to the neoliberal capitalist global order? Why is it he contends, that the discourse of capitalist development is so familiar and pervasive that it leaves us "embarrassingly empty-handed when trying to come up with a different view of things?" Is it because, as Gibson-Graham have argued, the neoliberal global order has consolidated itself not so much through institutional initiatives, but through our inability to conceptualize anything different?

> "Perhaps a global regime is consolidating itself not so much through institutional initiatives but through subjects who experience themselves as increasingly subsumed to a global order—enter here the world economic system, known also as the market, or neoliberalism, or capitalism.

Becoming part of the imagined global community involves our subjection to this order, our (re)constitution not primarily as national citizens
but as economic subjects—productive or less so, competitive or not, winning or losing on the economic terrain" (Gibson-Graham, 2003, p.49).

As a testament to the difficulty in conceptualizing alternatives to capitalist development, Gibson-Graham and Ruccio argue that even Escobar's
(1995) path-breaking attempt to deconstruct the development discourse
fails to break out of the logic of capitalism. Escobar seeks to conceptualize
alternatives and yet fails to dislodge capitalist practices from being the central point of reference. Escobar looks to new social movements as socially
embedded grassroots group that use culturally defined understandings of
the environment in their articulation of economic policymaking. However,
Gibson-Graham and Ruccio point out that these movements, hailed as they
are for local visions of reconstructing civil society, are inevitably represented as small, marginal groups that are taking on "The Global Forces of
Capitalism." This, the authors observe, is "capitalocentric," whereby capitalism is the "center," or central reference, and other economic formations
are defined in terms of their relation to it. Thus, capitalism is rendered as
an ontological given, a container that "holds" social totality and is thus
beyond discussion dispute (Gibson-Graham and Ruccio, 2001). By placing
capitalism in the "center" and local economic formations at "the margins,"
post-development theory is self-defeating in that local groups are portrayed
as weak and insignificant next to global capitalism and therefore unlikely
to survive or make a difference as rather exceptional cases. "Rather than
representing the economy as a radically heterogeneous social space, post-
development critics reinforce the discursive hegemony of capitalism and
thereby tend to marginalize the very alternative economic practices they
seek to promote" (Gibson-Graham and Ruccio, 2001, p.164).

How can we acknowledge the existence of alternative forms of society and economy, especially in the Third World, without referring to them
as backwards and primitive vis-à-vis capitalist practices? In other words,
how can we conceptualize the economy, economic processes and relations,
without using capitalist processes as the central point of reference? The
challenge is to question the very epistemological underpinnings of capitalism. If global capitalism appears to be "disproportionately powerful by the
virtue of its indisputable reality," it is, Gibson-Graham and Ruccio suggest,
because of our inability to theorize any other reality.

What if we conducted a simple "thought experiment," Gibson-Graham (1993) ask (in their provocatively titled piece, *How to Smash Capitalism while Working at Home in Your Spare Time*), and theorized the

capitalist economy not as something unified, autonomous and all-encompassing, but as something fragmented, heterogeneous and inhabited by groups of people with diverse economic practices and cultural constructions? In other words, what if we conceptualized capitalism as something small dispersed and fragmented and recognized that capitalist institutions have to continually negotiate their existence among a diversity of non-capitalist practices and cultural constructions?[8] Any historical, contextual and institutional analysis of developing countries show that local practices always exist and mediate the various forms of capitalisms that may arise, since every capitalist economy is colored by the specific history, culture and geography of the particular country.

Moreover, when global capitalism encounters indigenous non-capitalist economic forms, development discourse brings them into the fold of a teleological[9] vision of development by depicting them as "pre-capitalist" forms that either exist within the "pores" of global capitalism or "complement" it (Gibson-Graham and Ruccio, 2001). This discursive depiction of local economic practices as being either "primitive," "marginal" and ultimately unlikely to survive serves to reinforce the view of them as being "backwards" (a teleological move), "traditional" practices that may be residual for the moment but will eventually die out. On the other hand, global capitalism is portrayed as powerful, progressive-where progress means change for the better—and if not for the better, then anyway relentless and unstoppable (Gibson-Graham, 1993).

A STRING OF PROPOSITIONS

I end this introductory section by summarizing my intentions. Like the above-mentioned authors, I want to recognize that economic practices worldwide are diverse—and not just capitalist.[10] For the purposes of this dissertation, I will focus on economic practices in Egypt (this is the subject of Chapter four). Recognizing the economy as being characterized by a heterogeneity of context-specific practices is to me, an important move towards re-conceptualizing development as something that does not necessarily take the form of industrialization, urbanization and mass commodification as experienced by the United States and Europe. This chapter therefore, attempts to provide the epistemological basis for this project, arguing that there are connections between the practices of participatory research and postmodern theory. I find that practitioners of participatory research, postmodern theorists as well as many anthropologists all share a worldview that is different than that of mainstream economics, a view that is referred to as "social constructivism." Social constructivists take an epistemological stance that lends itself to discursive and dialectical ways of creating knowledge and hence policymaking. In arguing for this way of creating knowledge, I will make the following string of arguments:

> Argument 1: The economics that informs development policymakers is an economics of an essentialist epistemology in that it presumes that any "apparent complexity can be analyzed to reveal a simplicity lying at its core" (Resnick and Wolff, 1987).

I begin by addressing the issue of why I think an epistemological critique is important. What is the relationship between thinking and being, and between the individual and society?[11] How does a discipline legitimize the knowledge that it produces? In this section I will discuss the epistemological stance underlying mainstream economic theory and argue that it is "essentialist." The following sections will illustrate how a paradigm's response to these fundamental questions has far-reaching policy implications.[12]

> Argument 2: In this section I will illustrate the influence of "essentialism" for development policies, such as the notion that certain policies can be applied throughout the world because all economies are characterized by universal laws and principles.

> Argument 3: Essentialism is also apparent in the underlying vision of development that takes a teleological view progress: the story of humankind told by the discourse of economic development is a metanarrative of an essence that moves ever forward through history. For development, this is reflected in the notion that all economies will eventually move through a process of industrialization, technological revolution and urbanization, and that this process of modernization is, if not for the better, then anyway inevitable.[13] The belief in this preordained end, or telos, underlies the inability to conceptualize development without economic growth, and the accompanying questions in the literature as to why the economic growth rates of countries have failed to "converge."

> Argument 4: By contrast, social constructivism subscribes to a non-essentialist or postmodern epistemology. By honoring "the specificity of every site, practice and conjecture" (Resnick and Wolff, 1987), postmodern ways of knowing create a space in which we can reassert the value of alternative experiences and ways of knowing.

Argument 5: Postmodern theorists point out that not only is knowledge socially constructed, but also the production of knowledge is inseparable from the exercise of power. The work of Michel Foucault for instance, has been instrumental in showing the discourses are not neutral with respect to the social and natural phenomena they are describing. Rather, through their narrative, they "effectively construct, regulate and control knowledge, social relations and institutions" (Kellner, 1992). Drawing on Foucault, Escobar (1995) shows how the narrative of economic development discursively colonized Third World nations, willing them to accept "price of massive impoverishment, of selling Third World resources to the most convenient bidder, of degrading their physical and human ecologies, of condemning their indigenous populations to near extinction" (p.92). The Third World he argues, was "made" to "think of themselves as inferior, underdeveloped and ignorant and to doubt the value of their own culture" (ibid).

Argument 6: By carrying out participatory research work development practitioners are attempting to operationalize a social constructivist epistemology. Without preconceived, historicist notions of progress and belief in technological solutions to poverty, "development becomes a project not of replication (of the experience of the West) but of exploration and invention."

Argument 1: The economics that informs policymakers is an economics of an essentialist epistemology, in that it presumes that any "apparent complexity can be analyzed to reveal a simplicity lying at its core"

"I do not regard positivism as a useless or silly movement. In its day it did good . . . it has become oppressive" (McCloskey, 1985)

I begin by addressing the issue of why I think an epistemological critique is important. How does a theory make sense of the world? What is its conceptual starting point? What is the relationship between theory and reality and between the individual and society? In the following pages, I will try to show that mainstream development theory is "modernist" in the sense that it is characterized by the search for an "essence"—a starting point, a logic or a capital t "Truth"—as well as a predetermined end, or "telos." Theories that are characterized by the search for this causal essence are variously referred to as "essentialist," "foundationalist" or "reductionist" because of their tendency to presume that "any apparent complexity—a person, a relationship, a historical occurrence and so forth—can be analyzed to reveal a simplicity at its core" (Resnick and Wolff, 1987). That is, essentialism is the epistemological stance that among the multitude of phenomena that may be involved in explaining an occurrence, some are considered to be inessential and others essential causes. The objective of theories that are essentialist therefore, is to find and express this causal essence.

The search for this essence has framed numerous questions in the discourse of economics. I will focus on the following two: in the way a theory legitimizes its claims to "Truth" and in the way that a theory conceptualizes the social totality.

Epistemology, Ontology: how Truth is determined

How does a theory make sense of the world? Classical ontology holds that the world is divided into two distinct and separate realms: thinking (the realm of theory) and reality (the realm of being) (Cullenberg, 1999). According to this ontological structure of the world, the knowing subject exists independent of the world and hence reality is potentially knowable, and there is the possibility of "True" knowledge. This ontological view gives rise to the epistemological question: how do we close the ontological gap between theory and reality? Or, how do we know what we know?

For rationalists such as Rene Descartes, we know what we know through introspection: our knowledge of the world is based on a priori reason.[14] That is, the human mind (with its deductive abilities) is adequate to apprehend the world because like the world, the mind is organized according to a rational structure and this structure embodies certain universal principles. Theory therefore, is capable of expressing "the conceptual essence of reality" (Resnick and Wolff, 1987). Unlike rationalists, empiricists such as David Hume, John Locke and John Stuart Mill, held the view that experience rather than reason is the source of knowledge. To them, the mind was a tabular rasa—a blank slate. As the world unfolds, the mind observes and collects theories, and these theories capture or condense the underlying essence or truth of reality.[15]

Starting with the position that world exists separate and distinct from us, how do we differentiate between which theories are good and which are bad at expressing the underlying truth or essence of reality? In other words, how do we evaluate competing theories? This is the project of positivism, to demarcate between good and bad theories, or science and non-science.[16] Numerous economists (Amariglio, 1980; McCloskey, 1985; Screpanti, 2001) have been arguing for years that most of their profession has been preaching—if not practicing—a modernist,[17] positivist view of the world, such as advocated by Milton Friedman in *The Methodology of Positive Economics*. Positivism draws on both the traditions of empiricism and rationalism: human minds are not simply tabular rasas, but are tainted with innate ideas, and some ideas are intuitive while others are observed. The methodology of positivism calls for building up our knowledge of the world based on "facts," where these facts are "objective representations of reality" (Dow, 2001). It calls for reproducible experiments, hypothesis testing, prediction and control—all carried out in a disinterested fashion, because the subject is thought to be able to separate herself from the object of her study.

In sum, the ontological and epistemological position of positivism allows that there is the possibility for a True knowledge of the world, and that it has developed the method to at least get close to this truth.

An alternative to the dual ontological structure of the world described above, is that of social constructivists such as Kuhn, Althusser, Derrida, Feyerabend, Foucault, McCloskey and Resnick and Wolff. Their understanding of "How do we know what we know" rejects the ontological gap between thinking and being. Our thoughts about the world, they stress, cannot be independent of the ways we experience or think about it. Instead they argue that thinking and being "mutually constitute one another" (Cullenberg, 1999). In other words, although the world exists independent of us, our knowledge of the world is contingent on the way we experience it. Therefore, for social constructivists, knowledge is something that is created (social constructivists are not idealists). Furthermore, the production of knowledge is contingent on the community of its producers (Kuhn, 1962) and meaning is "taken from context and conveyed by language"(Dow, 2001). Consequently, they stress the discursive nature of knowledge. Knowledge, says Feyerabend (1988) "resides in the ways we speak"; it is constituted by a plethora of forms such as lists, stories, dramatic accounts, histories; it is contingent on time and space, and "rigor" can come from any systematically laid out argument -"good science is good conversation," as McCloskey puts it.

> The objectivity of individuals . . . consists in their participation in the
> collective give-and-take of critical discussion and not in some special
> relation (of detachment hardheadedness) they may bear to their obser-
> vations. Thus understood, objectivity is dependent upon the depth and
> scope of the transformative interrogation that occurs in any given scien-
> tific community. This community-wide process ensures (or can ensure)
> that the hypothesis ultimately accepted as supported by some set of
> data do not reflect a single individual's idiosyncratic assumptions about

the natural world. To say that a theory or hypothesis was accepted on the basis of objective methods does not entitle us to say it is true but rather it reflects the critically achieved consensus of the scientific community (Helen Longino, 1990, p.79)

Objectivity for social constructivists lies not in transcendental claims to Truth or a god-like essence, but in conversations that may transform a community. Ultimately, social constructivists are epistemologically anti-essentialist: there cannot be one True way to know the world hence; to them reality is socially constructed and therefore, it is always already theory-laden.

Epistemology, Ontology and Social Totality: how theories explain causality

The search for an essence also underlies the way economic theory explains the relationship between individuals and society—or the social totality. Mainstream Neoclassical economic theory is based on the Cartesian social totality, the ontological structure of which consists of "a set of basic elements or atoms that exist prior to and independent from the totality" (Cullenberg, 1999). Following Descartes, in this view a totality such as nature or society is conceptualized as a machine made of independent parts (as opposed to an organic whole). The integrity of the "parts" of the totality imply that they are independent of their relationships to one another and to the "whole," and the whole is merely the interaction of the parts. For instance, in neoclassical economics, the totality of the economy is the sum total of the interaction of discrete, unrelated individuals.[18] This analytic, known as "methodological individualism,"[19] reduces the complexity of the economy to the rational economic agent homo economicus. The behavior of this social atom as it manifests itself though preferences, is then analyzed in consumer and producer theory as the causal force that underlies the mechanism of markets. Commodity prices, Neoclassical economists would explain, are "caused essentially by individual preferences and production technology" (Resnick and Wolff, 1987, p.3). Thus, the Cartesian totality is said to be reductionist, deterministic or essentialist because causal explanations can be ultimately reduced to an essence (such as individual rationality). The implications of the essentialism underlying methodological individualism for economics is, as Mark Blaug remarks, "devastating" (1983, p.46): "In effect, it would rule out all macroeconomic propositions that cannot be reduced to microeconomic ones, and since few have yet been so reduced, this amounts in turn to saying goodbye to almost whole of received macroeconomics" (ibid).

In opposition to an essentialist epistemological standpoint is that of "overdetermination," first conceptualized by Althusser and further developed by Resnick and Wolff (1987).[20] This de-centered notion of a social totality rejects the essentialism of methodological individualism espoused by the Cartesian totality. Instead of reducing the social totality to the sum of independently constituted parts, an overdetermined totality is one where the parts mutually constitute one another and are themselves a product of their cultural, spatial and temporal contexts (Cullenberg, 1999). An overdetermined explanation of causality therefore, rejects the search for a causal essence or logical structure of the world. If all aspects of a society mutually constitutes one another, then a phenomenon such as individual behavior cannot be reduced to an essence such as rationality, because individual behavior is the expression of a host of socialization processes that are contingent on social constructions such as gender, ethnicity, class, religion and history etc. Analyzing social phenomena based only on rational individual behavior therefore is an essentialist move that reduces a complex, overdetermined process by ignoring the impact of other non-economic socialization processes.[21]

> Antiessentialism is the rejection of any presumption that complexities are reducible to simplicities of the case-and effect type. Instead the presumption is that every element in the context of any event plays its distinctive role in determining that event. Every cause is itself also an effect and vice versa. An antiessentialist or nonreductionist theory refuses refuses to look for the essential cause of any event because it does not presume that it exists. An antiessentialist theory understands that every theory (including itself) to be inherently partial, a particularly focused intervention in social discourse (Resnick and Wolff, 1987, p.3).

Given the diversity of societies, the acknowledgement of such complexities has led many to reject an overdetermined epistemology and argue that such a stance leads to cultural relativism and hence critical paralysis. However, Postmodern theorists (and certain development practitioners as I will argue in the following pages) have argued that an overdetermined epistemological stance may be perceived as critically paralyzing only if the object of theory is to simplify complex social phenomena in the search for causal essences and "True" knowledge of the world. If on the other hand, the object of theory is to produce knowledge that is context-specific, then the methodology of knowledge creation should involve careful analysis of each situation, case by case. The overarching objective then becomes not to apply universal laws and principles based on standardized axioms, but to understand a particular phenomenon as being affected by various cultural, historical as well as economic processes:

> Overdetermination is a form of relativism to be sure, but that does not imply a quietude, whether scholarly or politically (if you want to separate them out). It does imply, I think, an attention to case study and the specificity of each analysis as done by institutionalist econo- mists and not the strategy of empirical work as is classically done with econometrics, which tries to separate distinct explanatory factors and weight or sign them. (Cullenberg, 1999, p.814)

To conclude this section, there are three key implications of an essen- tialist epistemological stance for the field of development economics. First, epistemologically essentialist theories desire to attain ineffable or transcen- dental "Truths" about the world. Theories that follow a specific definition of scientific methodology (and that have not been falsified) are thought to be closer approximations to "Truth," and these are to be distinguished from those that are not (non-scientific). Thus an essentialist epistemological stance effectively prevents knowledge that is not based on a positivist meth- odology of science from influencing development policymaking.

A second consequence of an essentialist viewpoint is that of the Carte- sian totality, which often depends on the assumption that human behavior is, for the most part, based on rational calculations.[22] This has reduced all social phenomena to the calculation of self-interest that is characteristic of market transactions. Related to this point is the third implication of essen- tialism for development economics—that of economic determinism. This is the theoretical move by economists to ascribe a privileged position to economic explanations over other forms of explanations such as cultural, religious and historical ones, to describe social outcomes.[23] By privileging economic forces in describing causality, mainstream economists are pro- moting the (modernist) view that "most if not all areas of contemporary life are prone to the logic of capital and mostly to the vagaries of market forces" (Cullenberg et. al, 2001, p.7). Conversely, postmodern theorists have reclaimed the significance of non-capitalist, non-market domains by showing that local economies are embedded in diverse social institutions that have evolved in specific cultural, spatial and historical contexts.[24]

Argument 2: "The master's tools cannot dismantle the master's house"

> "Once it is recognized that individuals respond to incentives, and that market failure is the result of inappropriate incentives rather than of

non-responsiveness, the separateness of development economics as a field largely disappears" (Anne Krueger, 1986)

How do we know what we know about economic development? The above quotation appears to take the stand that development economics is a branch of applied economics. Its underlying metaphor is that of a machine (the economy) that can be reduced to its constituent component parts (individuals). These "parts" of the machine are implicitly identical (all individuals are rational) and interact with each other in the same way (all rational individuals will react similarly to incentives). Therefore, since all economies are composed of rational individuals, who will respond identically to incentives, their behavior can be generalized into economic laws that must apply across all countries. Although this is a simplification, it is not too far from the weltanshaung implicit in the "Washington Consensus": the package of policy measures known as stabilization and structural adjustment, are based on the implicit assumption that all economies (and their basic components, individuals) are similar and will respond similarly to market incentives (Kenny and Williams, 2000).

For development theory, the epistemological position that the true nature of the economy can be observed, enumerated and generalized into universal laws means that all economic processes everywhere are, in principle knowable, and that these laws ultimately govern economies irrespective of time and space. In the context of development economics, this methodological drive to explain social phenomena by formulating universal laws (similar to the methodology of natural scientists to explain natural phenomenon) took the form of mathematical equations that purported to describe the process of economic growth.[25] "For many years," remarks Michael Todaro, "conventional wisdom equated development almost exclusively with the rapidity of national output growth" (1997, page104). The logic underlying growth theories was that increased national savings and investment would leader to faster rates of economic growth and hence development. Increased saving and investment may be necessary conditions for economic growth, but they are only two out of a multitude of factors that are needed to bring about not only growth, but also the much more societal phenomenon of development. The logic that increased investment leads to economic growth and hence development was based on the experience of the war-ravaged European nations under the Marshall Plan in the aftermath of the Second World War. As Todaro notes,

The Marshall Plan worked for Europe because the European countries receiving aid possessed the necessary structural, institutional and attitudinal conditions (e.g. well-integrated commodity and money markets, highly developed transport facilities, a well trained and educated workforce, the motivation to succeed, an efficient government bureaucracy) to convert new capital effectively into higher levels of output. The Rostow and Harrod-Domar models implicitly assume the existence of these same attitudes and arrangements in underdeveloped nations. Yet in many cases they are lacking, as are complementary factors such as managerial competence, skilled labor, and the ability to plan and administer a wide assortment of development projects (Todaro, 1997, p.75).

Furthermore, despite the heterogeneity of economies, their initial conditions and their growth processes, theories of economic growth are marked by the search for some causal essence. "What factors are needed for economic growth?" Over time, growth theory has privileged different variables as the significant causal force, starting with physical capital accumulation (Ragnar Nurkse, 1950s, Harrod-Domar, 1972), the rate of technological change (Robert Solow, 1957), human capital (Robert Lucas, 1988), back to physical capital in endogenous growth theory (Romer, 1993) and then to institutional reform in the late 1990s following the work of Ronald Coase (1937), Demsetz (1967), Douglass North (1990) and Oliver Williamson (1999).[26] "Development" says Watts (1995) "has rarely broken free from organicist notions of growth and from close a close affinity with teleological views of history, science and progress."

Argument 3: Tied to essentialism is a modernist teleological view of history and progress

Descartes' metaphor of society as a machine that could be explained by the actions of its parts or individuals also resonates with the Enlightenment philosophy of theoretical humanism. Giving precedence to the individual (as opposed to God or the Church) as the ultimate site of sovereignty, theoretical humanism invoked "Man's" ability to reason as his way to achieve "True" knowledge and hence mastery over the world.

Man's ability to separate himself from Nature, reason from emotion, thinking from being, and to separate himself from the object of his study, allowed him to potentially grasp the "true" nature of the world. This scientific method of apprehending the world was to bring about progress as "truth drove out error and knowledge replaced ideology" (Cullenberg et. al, 2001, p.9). For development, just as liberal democracy promised individual rights and freedom from political oppression, so scientific knowledge embodied in economic growth promised freedom from poverty, hunger, early mortality and a better quality of life in general. More specifically, modernization theory held that the only solution for "underdeveloped" nations was to follow the trajectory of agricultural revolution, urbanization, industrialization and mass commodification as already experienced in the West. This historicist, teleological view of development is illustrated clearly by this passage from Walt Rostow's The Stages of Economic Growth: A Non-Communist Manifesto (1960).

> It is possible to identify all societies in their economic dimensions, as lying within one of five categories: the traditional society, the pre-conditions for take-off into self-sustaining growth, the take-off, the drive to maturity, and the age of high mass consumption. . . . These stages are not merely descriptive. They are not merely a way of generalizing certain factual observations about the sequence of development of modern societies. They have an inner logic and continuity. . . . They constitute, in the end, both a theory about economic growth and a more general, if still highly partial theory about modern history as a whole (Walt Rostow, pages 1, 3 ,4 and 12, 1960).

Although the developed world's experience development policy-making was at this point, limited to the implementation of the Marshall Plan in Europe, they also drew on their own historical experience of transformation from impoverished agrarian subsistence societies to modern industrial giants. "Was it not true that all modern industrial nations were once underdeveloped agrarian societies?" (p.71). Todaro goes on to remark that

> The logic and simplicity of these two strands of thought -(the utility of massive injections of capital and the historical pattern of the now developed countries—was too irresistible to be refuted by scholars, politicians, and administrators in rich countries to whom people and ways of life in the Third World were often no more real than U.N. statistics or scattered chapter in anthropology books (ibid).

Argument 4: That social constructivist theory offers a non-essentialist way of looking at things and that for development economics, postmodernism's emphasis on knowledge as discourse creates a "space."

By rejecting the existence of an ontological gap between thinking and being, social constructivism rejects the ability of theory to express some underlying Truth or essence of reality. If the subject or creator of a theory cannot be separated from her experience of reality, then truth or knowledge is reflects her particular experiences. Hence, given the varied experiences of communities, there is the possibility of many truths (as opposed to just one universal Truth). The creation of knowledge therefore is subject to context, culture, time and space because the individual in an overdetermined social totality is the site of various different historical, cultural, gendered and class-based processes. Knowledge therefore, is created not by searching for a universal Truth, but through the dialectical processes of different communities coming into contact with one another's truths. Postmodern theorists argue that the nature of knowledge is discursive and not scientific in the positivist sense of the word.

If the nature of knowledge is discursive (even economists with their laws, mathematical proofs and regressions are really just trying to get others to listen, says McCloskey(1985)), and if discourse is context specific and "space, time, reality change when we move from one language to another" (Feyerabend, 1988), then postmodernism allows for a space where other "non-sciensical" forms of knowledge can be acknowledged. If knowledge is not neutral, unbiased, objective or capable of reflecting absolute "truths," but rather contingent on local realities and subject to people's race, gender and class, then it is context-specific and cannot necessarily be transmitted to other localities. "In sum," Escobar (1995) contends, the belief that theory is produced in one place and applied to another is no longer acceptable practice." Under positivism, the purpose of theory was two-fold: to develop a true picture of the world, and to gain some measure of control over it. Postmodernism gives up the notion of universal truth, arguing instead "the truth for a given community is what works to serve the self-defined needs of that community" (Hoksbergen, 1994).

Argument 5: Not only is knowledge socially constructed, but the production of knowledge is inseparable from the exercise of power

Economist's preoccupation with positivism and the Popperian demarcation criterion as to what does and does not constitute knowledge has been particularly harmful for the intended beneficiaries of development. By subscribing to the epistemological position that it is possible to arrive at neutral, objective, "scientific knowledge" of the world, positivism has silenced forms of knowledge that are considered "non-scientific." It has, says Escobar (1997), established

> a discursive practice that sets the rules of the game: who can speak, from what points of view, with what authority, and according to what criteria of expertise; it sets the rules that must be followed for this or that problem, theory or object to emerge and be named, analyzed, and eventually transformed into a policy or plan (p.87).

In rejecting the epistemological stance that there is true knowledge or that knowledge can be objective, social constructivists raise questions about the nature of knowledge-production process itself. Whom does theory serve? Who speaks? Whose voice is heard? Whose voice is not heard? Who decides what does or does not constitute knowledge? In other words, social constructivists such as Foucault (1980) have called to attention that the creation of scientific knowledge is inseparable from the exercise of power.

> What types of knowledge do you want to disqualify in the instant of your demand: "Is it science?" Which speaking discoursing subjects - which subjects of experience and knowledge -do you then want to diminish when you say "I who conduct this discourse am conducting a scientific discourse, and I am a scientist"? (Foucault, 1980, p.85)

More importantly, Foucault argues that if knowledge is inseparable from power, then it cannot be uninterested. Power, he contends, is "that which represses" (ibid, p.90), and the academic preoccupation with what does and does not constitute knowledge effectively acts as a structure that gives power (the ability to repress) to some voices over others.

Drawing on the works of Foucault (1980) and Said (1979, 1993), Escobar has been instrumental in showing how the production of the discourse of development is inseparable from the exercise of Western power. His textual analysis of the development discourse shows how "underdevelopment," like Said's "Orientalism," is something that is produced by the Western imaginary: "Development proceeded by creating abnormalities ('the poor,' 'the malnourished,' 'the illiterate,' 'the landless') which it would treat or reform. Seeking to eradicate all problems, it actually ended up multiplying them indefinitely" (Escobar, 1995, p.214).

Thus, an epistemological analysis of the discourse of economic development yields two separate implications. First, the notion that the subject exists separate and distinct from the object of her study may lead to problematic conclusions about what does and does not constitute true knowledge. Second, that historically in development economics, the subject (or the person creating knowledge) has occupied specific class, race and gender positions while the objects of study (the poor, the illiterate) have been denied subjectivity.[27] In other words, the ontological subject/object divide has created a hierarchy with fixed notions of "truth" and fixed structures of power.

By contrast, much of the work by anthropologists, institutional economists and practitioners of participatory research show that individuals and communities continually negotiate power structures so that wherever there is power, there is resistance (Hoodfar, 1999 and Singerman, 2000). These contextual studies recognize that local economic practices are sites where power is sometimes resisted and re-appropriated through the production of context-specific knowledge, or discourse: For if it is true that the majority of people live within structures of domination that are not their own making, it is also true that they participate in these structures, adapting, resisting, transforming or subverting them through manifold tactics (Escobar, 1995).

An epistemological stance that wished to reflect these local realities, by conceptualizing truth and power as fluid categories cannot, therefore, restrict itself to positivist ways of creating knowledge. Instead, social constructivists argue, the creation of knowledge must emphasize the discursive nature of the knowledge creation process that is dialectical (as opposed to hierarchical notions of science versus non-science) so that power structures are always contingent on dialogue and persuasion (as opposed to the search for an underlying essence or truth).

Argument 6: By carrying out participatory research work development practitioners are attempting to operationalize a social constructivist epistemology

The ideological roots of participatory research go back to the work of Paolo Freire (1968) who advocated mobilizing local communities to challenge existing political regimes in northeastern Brazil. The various techniques of doing participatory research -Participatory Rural Appraisal (PRA), Participatory Action Research (PAR) and Rapid Rural Appraisal (RRA) -coalesced in the late 1980s to early 1990s from a number of sources. Chambers (1997) cites five different field-oriented disciplines that have contributed to the methodology of participatory research:

i)   Action-reflection research: inspired by Freire's Pedagogy of the Oppressed (1968), this stream of thought stressed the view that the poor are capable of conducting their own research and analysis and should be empowered and enabled to do so. Initially popular in Latin America, participatory action research has also spread to Tanzania, India, Bangladesh and the United States.

ii) Agro-ecosystems analysis: initially developed by Conway (1985, 1986, 1987) in Thailand, the techniques of agro-ecosystems analysis have become immensely popular for supplementing traditional questionnaires. A combination of systems analysis and ecological thinking, it uses studies of time (seasonal calendars, long term trends), space (maps, transects), flow charts (Venn diagrams, causal flows) and decision-making (decision trees) to analyze issues such as sustainability, equity and productivity.

iii) Applied anthropology: the work of Rhoades (1982) in Peru has been influential in advocating that fieldwork should be a flexible art rather than scientific, that the researcher should live in the field, establish rapport and be mindful of learning indigenous technical knowledge from the community.

iv) Field Research on farming systems: Richards(1985), Bunch (1985) were among the first to document that farmers conducted their own experiments, assessments and analysis of farming systems that appeared to be unsystematic from an outside viewpoint.

v) Rapid Rural appraisal: RRA evolved in the late 70s and early 80s in response to the realization that "development experts" were urban based professionals who would make a brief visit to the community to gather data with which to formulate policies. They were "outsiders" who extracted information that they thought were pertinent to formulate what they thought were appropriate policies. Moreover, the most common form of extracting information, surveys, were not only difficult and costly to carry out, but were also unavoidably ridden with errors and misrepresentations of the community in question. In response to these problems RRA experimented with alternative ways of gathering information.

Thus, practitioners in these fields came to a number of realizations. At an obvious level, there were projects that failed because they did not account for local customs, or that they did not take advantage of local expertise and indigenous forms of knowledge.[28] Out of this awareness, they began consulting with community members on indigenous technology before considering the introduction of modern technology into their environment. This led to the recognition that communities had their own analytical frameworks and ways of knowing -that they were not only more capable but more efficient at conducting their own research and analysis. Moreover, the local realities they expressed were frequently of conditions, problems, livelihood strategies and priorities that were beyond the conceptual framework of development professionals.[29]

Initially the research process remained (and in many cases still remains[30]) extractive in nature: researchers come into a community, elicit information, write up their reports without it necessarily benefiting the community (Chambers, 1994; 1997). Gradually however, a sea change occurred, when practitioners became sensitive to the power dynamics involved:

Villagers . . . have learned to confirm what they know the question-
ers expect to hear. This is not only through politeness and awareness
that the truth will be met with incredulity, but also through the desire
to maintain good relations with authoritative outsiders who may bring
as yet unknown benefits; a school, road or advantageous recognition of
the village, for example (Leach and Fairhead, 1994).

They realized that to break the donor-recipient syndrome and
empower local communities, development professionals have to hand over
the power—"adopt humility and hand over the stick"—in the policymaking
process (Chambers, 1997). At that point, the role of the researcher changes
from being the creator of knowledge to that of merely a facilitator. Frequently, a successful facilitator initiates a process of participatory analysis
and "sits back, or walks away" (Chambers, 1994) allowing the community
to "own" the policymaking process, determining what is on the agenda,
how to go about obtaining and organizing information and how to use it.

The sea-change involved here is that successful challenges to "top-
down" to policymaking require fundamental changes in research strategy.
Participatory approaches that allow local communities to establish their
own analytical frameworks can thus be part of a broader goal to shape
popular movements in pressing for social and political change. In the final
analysis therefore, participatory research has to do with the attitude of the
"outside" researcher and the approach they take to the research process. "If
PRA approaches are so powerful and popular," Chambers points out, the
puzzle is why it has taken until the 1990s for them to emerge . . . Much
of the mystery disappears if we look for explanations not in local people
but in ourselves, as outsider professionals" (Chambers, 1997, p.128).

To this end, Chambers, as well as others such as Holland and Blackburn (1998), Moser (1998) and Uphoff (1992) have been instrumental
in raising a series of questions: Whose voice is heard in the policymaking
process? Whose reality is represented? Whose knowledge counts? Who
changes?

*Conclusion: Empower (em pou'ər) -1. to give power or authority to; to
authorize, esp by legal or official means 2. To enable or permit (Webster's
Encyclopedic Unabridged Dictionary of the English Language)*

Following the work of Cullenberg, Amariglio, Ruccio, and McCloskey, in
this chapter I have argued that mainstream economics is positivist. A vari-
ant of modernism, positivist concepts of theorizing have called for simplify-
ing, standardizing axioms, laws and universal principles that downplay the
significance of time, space, culture, as well as social constructions of human

identity. Postmodern theorizing on the other hand emphasizes a dialectical way of creating knowledge -a way that encourages conversation between and among cultures.

An emphasis on the discursive and not just the scientific nature of knowledge and the recognition that knowledge is context-specific should then ground policymaking in local realities and interpretations. Development practitioners argue that who better to express "complex, diverse, dynamic and unpredictable local realities" than local communities? (Chambers 1994 and 1997; Holland and Blackburn, 1998)

Despite being fraught with difficulties, I find that participatory research has the potential to play a role that goes beyond augmenting and complementing the positivist research paradigm that continues to dominate the economics profession. The dialectical nature of participatory research lends itself to discussions on indigenous knowledge and contextual realities that allow for the possibility of alternative concepts of development to emerge. More importantly, the dialogue between development practitioners and local communities has helped raise awareness of the power structure involved in the dichotomy between the researcher and the object of her research. As Foucault (1980) argues, the creation of knowledge cannot be separated from the exercise of power: "Modern humanism is therefore mistaken in drawing this line between knowledge and power. Knowledge and power are integrated with one another, and there is no point in dreaming of a time when knowledge will cease to depend on power; this is just a way of reviving humanism in a utopian guise"(1980, p.52). The challenge therefore is to maintain a constant vigilance, or critical self-awareness during the knowledge creation process.

Participation in the policymaking process is an old notion, going as far back as the 1960s in Paolo Freire's work. However, this paper has argued that despite fashionable rhetoric, development policymaking is still bound to an essentialist, reductivist epistemology and that there is a disregard for local voice, expertise and knowledge. The techniques of participatory research can be easily incorporated into traditional policymaking to add participatory component to the programming cycle. However, I have argued in this chapter that the full ramifications of truly participatory research go further than the "add participation and stir" approach.[31]

Chapter Three
The Political Economy of Participation in Egypt

INTRODUCTION

What has been the historical experience of participation in Egypt? How are the fruits of the development process shared among the members of the Egyptian society? An inescapable aspect of modernity in Egypt is the palpable presence of the State in everyday life. Historically, the modern Egyptian state has exercised considerable influence over both the political and economic spheres of participation. The institutions of the modern nation-state that normally involve collective action—such as political parties, labor unions and the media—are monitored, censored and effectively controlled by the Ministry of Information. Since 1964, by law civic associations have to be formally approved by the State. Community-based or non-government organization that have not registered with the Ministry of Information are considered illegal. "Those who consciously resist the state or who engage in conflict with statist objectives" notes Singerman, "are rarely free of fears and anxieties about possible retribution" (Singerman, 1997, p. 3).

State control over the economic sphere was officially instituted beginning in 1960. The large-scale nationalization that took place in 1961 effectively restricted the private sector to agriculture, real estate and the informal sectors, but even these sectors were subject to price controls and centralized controls over marketing, raw materials and foreign exchange (Hansen, 1975; Abdel Fadil, 1980). State-owned enterprises monopolized the banking sector, the manufacturing sector, foreign trade as well as the bulk of the transportation sector. Thus, until fairly recently, the public sector has been the main engine of growth, the vehicle of state-led industrialization, and responsible for the major part of new investment and employment.[1]

Today, Egypt continues to be characterized as a predominantly "social-ist" economy that is now, through the privatization of public enterprises and liberalization of markets, transitioning into a market-based economy. However, class analysis suggests that the predominant way of organizing economic activities in the public sector have been state-*capitalist* in nature.

In public enterprises of the key industrial sectors such as manufacturing and petroleum, workers did not participate in shop-floor decision-making. A state-appointed board of directors—appropriated the surplus labor per-formed by public sector employees and decided how it should be distributed. Under the so-called era of "Arab socialism" therefore, the performers of sur-plus labor were excluded from participating in the appropriation and distri-bution of this surplus. In terms class analytical terms, the class processes that has constituted Egyptian public enterprises are capitalist in nature. They are referred to as "state-capitalist." If the public enterprise distributes its output in commodity form then this economic endeavor is consistent with market activity. Since the monetary value of the physical product of surplus labor (or surplus *value*) is appropriated by someone other than the person who produced it, public sector employees are said to be in an *exploitative* relation with the State. In other words, the predominant way of organizing economic activity within public enterprises, state-*capitalism*, has excluded people from participating in the decisions that affected their work, the workplace and more generally, the realm of distributive justice.

Disenfranchised by an autocratic regime and excluded by state-capital-ist class processes, what has been the historical experience of participation in this politically and economically repressive context? What does participation in the development process mean today in the era of "market reforms"? The first part of this chapter explores the historical experience of development and participation in the context of macroeconomic policies implemented by the State. It finds that historically, participation in the development process has been restricted to the parameters of Egypt's social contract: economic entitlements in return for forgoing political representation. The second part of the chapter examines the experience of participation and development in light of the gradual dismantling of this social contract and the adoption of comprehensive market reforms in 1991. It finds that the effects of capi-talist economic growth in Egypt continues to be uneven, exacerbating the huge regional disparities that today manifest themselves in a) severe human deprivation in the southern part of—or "Upper"—Egypt and b) a burgeon-ing informal sector that remains outside the purview of mainstream devel-opment policies. When addressing these exclusionary effects of capitalist growth however, dominant ideas of participation in the development process remain within a binary, moribund framework of either participation through the redistributive strategies of an interventionist state or participation as access to markets. In doing so, it fails to engage the ways in which local communities have carved out their own spaces of participation. The discussion in this chapter provides the macroeconomic background for the case studies in Chapters Four and Five.

STATE CAPITALISM AND THE POLITICAL ECONOMY OF PARTICIPATION IN EGYPT

Since 1956, the modern Egyptian state has been ruled by a succession of "weak military autocrats" (Bent Hansen, 1991).[2] Participation in the development process in Egypt has been characterized by unspoken arrangement between the State and the general populace. Although the nature of this arrangement has been changing, the "social compact" (Hansen, 1991) between the state and the Egyptian people, outlined in Gamal Abdel Nasser's 1962 Social Charter, continues to have a determining influence over the state's economic policy objectives. The tacit contract between the state and public has taken the form of "a *quid pro quo* exchange of political rights for entitlements" of basic goods and services and low-paid government jobs (Hansen, 1991; Springborg, 1989 and Roy, 1980).[3] In a 1962 speech outlining the Social Charter of Arab Socialism, Gamal Abdel Nasser emphasized "the right of each citizen to medical care, and then the right to receive education appropriate for his ability and talent. Then there is the right to an adequate job according with ability and education, together with a legally sanctioned minimum wage" (quoted in Said, 1972, p. 61). Since 1962 the state has guaranteed government employment for those with a secondary school diploma. A legacy of this policy today is that government jobs remain the fastest growing and the largest contributor to employment growth in the country (Ragui Assad, 1998). The *quid pro quo* exchange of political rights for entitlements led to subsidies for a variety of goods from basic foodstuffs to utilities such as electricity and water.[4]

Why haven't the economically dispossessed in Egypt risen up against the State? Partly because of the fear of brutal repercussions,[5] but also partly because of the limited redistributive strategy that has kept at bay the worst effects of poverty, inequality and its consequent material distress and political discontent.

> Egypt appears to be a relatively equitable society with reasonably good nutrition. Government, public enterprises, controls, and import

substitution seem to have been succeeding where private enterprise and free trade with a mix of export promotion and import substitution previously failed . . . It is a fact of life that naked feet and street beggars have virtually disappeared in Egypt. But the achievement in growth, equity and poverty in Egypt have been very uneven and their costs unnecessarily high (Hansen, 1991, p. 3).

The Infitah or "Open Door Policy" 1973–1986

President Anwar el Sadat's 1973 *October Paper* outlined Egypt's first reorientation away from Nasser's "Arab Socialism" towards a market economy through the *Infitah* or "Open Door Policy." The Open Door Policy called for promoting private sector investment, attracting foreign capital and technology, and looking to exports as the engine of long-run growth, jobs and prosperity. The cornerstone of the Open Door Policy was "Law No. 43 of 1974"which allowed tax concessions to foreign private firms in the form of tax holidays, exemptions from labor laws, import-export licenses and exchange rate control regulations. It distinguished between foreign investments in the "Free Zones" (such as Port Said) where tax holidays were indefinite and where joint ventures with local firms were not required, and inland projects, which required setting up partnerships with local firms. Despite attempts to attract foreign direct investment, the majority of projects implemented under Law No. 43 were undertaken by Egyptian private and public firms.[6]

What impact did these policies have on the development process in Egypt? Between 1974 and 1985, the economy grew at an unprecedented average rate of almost 8% per annum, fueled by a series of windfall rents however. Specific global conditions: high oil prices, Israel returning the Sinai oil fields, the reopening of the Suez Canal as well as remittances from Egyptian workers in neighboring Arab countries, created a huge influx of foreign exchange. In return, the State redistributed its increased revenue "to permit a politically motivated increase in consumption" (Hansen, 1991, p. 19). For those at the lower end of the income distribution, it increased its subsidy payments and continued the guaranteed employment scheme started under Nasser. For those at the upper end of the income distribution, the State in effect created the conditions for lucrative investment opportunities in imports. An overvalued exchange rate coupled with the creation of the Free Trade Zone of Port Said led to an exponential growth in imports of luxury goods. Competition from imported goods reduced the demand for domestically produced goods leading to underutilized capacity in domestic industry.

By redistributing the inflow of foreign exchange to fuel a domestic consumption boom, the State effectively secured its own conditions of existence. Hence, in spite of creating favorable conditions for private-capitalist class processes, state capitalist class-structures continued to dominate the economy. In seeking to secure its conditions of existence however, state policies exacerbated a series of macroeconomic imbalances that would ultimately lead to an internally generated set of contradictions.

Macroeconomic imbalances began to build up as increased levels of consumption along with relaxed restrictions on imports led to an increase in the demand for imported goods. The current account deficit doubled after the 1973 *Infitah*. Galal Amin (1995) notes that although some of this increase in imports consisted of much needed capital and intermediate goods for industrial production and for building infrastructure, much of it also consisted of "less necessary goods" such as "private motorcars" (ibid, p. 8). Furthermore, a third significant type of good that Egypt imported between 1977 and 1981 were military goods following the Camp David Accords and Sadat's role in the peace treaty with Israel in 1979. As Amin notes, "Arms purchases during those years were financed mainly by external borrowing at the very high commercial interest rates prevailing at that time. A 1984 IMF report mentions that military expenditures in Egypt increased at an annual rate of 20% in the years following 1979, reaching 32% in the last year of Sadat's rule" (ibid, p. 12).

Indeed, Amin argues that it was not so much the composition of imports that was harmful for Egypt's current account deficit and eventually foreign indebtedness, but the rates at which these loans were financed. What brought on the impending debt crisis for Egypt was the type of financing it used to buy these goods: "costly short term credit" and "at the very high commercial interest rates prevailing at the time" (ibid, p. 12). Imports soared and exports fell as the terms of trade deteriorated, mainly due to a four-fold rise in the price of US wheat imports between 1973–76. At the end of 1981, Egypt's foreign debt had amounted to more than 100% of its gross national product (Hansen, 1991, p. 200). External indebtedness would leave the State vulnerable to its creditors, to geopolitical instability and threaten its legitimacy at home. As Hansen notes, "In its inability to make ends meet Egypt has placed itself at the mercy of political designs and calculations of donors and international financiers" (Hansen, 1991, p. 5).

In 1977 under pressure from the IMF, the government proposed raising prices and food riots broke out in Cairo. Initially organized by skilled workers from the public sector, the rioting also drew in rural migrant workers who at this point had joined the ranks of the informal sector. Although the Cairo bread riot of 1977 subsided as soon as the government announced it would rescind the subsidy cuts, urban discontent continued to simmer.

1986–2003: The aftermath of the boom decade

As the government became increasingly indebted and was unable to finance its expenditure, Egypt became one of the most highly indebted countries in the world. In 1985 old outstanding debt fell due at a time that coincided with rising world interest rates as well as a drastic fall in oil prices. Egypt's foreign exchange receipts fell sharply, not only from the petroleum sector, but also from the Suez Canal and from labor remittances of Egyptian workers in the oil-rich countries. Unable to import intermediate goods, industry contracted; the inflation rate jumped from 13% in 1986 to 31% in 1987 (The WDI 1998). By the time the Gulf War broke out in 1991, Egypt's external debt stood at 150% of GDP, one of the highest debt levels in the world (Amin, 1995, p. 48). A series of agreements between the Government of Egypt and the International Monetary Fund provided debt relief in 1987 and then again in 1991 conditional on Egypt adopting "structural adjustment and stabilization policies.[7] The "Economic Reform and Structural Adjustment Program" (ERSAP) agreed to in 1991 called for privatizing the state-owned enterprises, liberalizing the trade sector and unifying the exchange rates, liberalizing the energy and transportation sectors and reducing the budget deficit through contractionary fiscal and monetary policies.

As the State itself admits however, the "Economic reforms during the 1990s were more concerned with stabilization, inflation and the balance of payments" than the other objectives of structural adjustment, such as improved standards of living (Ministry of Foreign Trade, 2004, p. 9). Although the State has successfully cut back its expenditures and reduced its external debt, the banking, oil, gas, insurance, and textiles sectors are still dominated by state-owned enterprises. The hardships associated with privatization are so high however, that Egyptian policy-makers have been delaying the process of privatizing the state-owned enterprises in the public sector for fear of political unrest (Posusney, 1997). Hence, despite lay-offs by public enterprises the government as a whole has increased its share of total employment, continuing its role as "the employer of the last resort" (Assad, 1999). The gradual implementation of market reforms since 1991 has been ascribed to the State's policy of "appeasement." On the one hand, the State has been appeasing international creditors (by selling off state-owned enterprises to the private sector for example). On the other hand, it continues to unofficially honor aspects of the past's social contract such as the guaranteed employment scheme for college graduates as a way to compensate for the lack of job growth in the economy.

Fifteen years after the onset of ERSAP and more than three decades of "opening" to western capital, technology and markets, a recurring theme in the literature is Egypt's failure to experience capitalist industrialization growth and development. Recurring questions vary along the lines of: "Why hasn't private sector investment been forthcoming in Egypt? Why haven't multinational companies been investing in Egypt despite government concessions since 1974? Why haven't 15 years of market reforms in agriculture brought about the large scale, mechanized "modern" (capitalist) farming with high yields and high value crops for exporting? Why hasn't the Egyptian economy experienced the agrarian transformation, urbanization, proletarization that are characteristic of advanced industrialized countries?" For many economists the answer to many of Egypt's economic problems is the fact that investments have not been forthcoming from private sector capitalists:

> Despite the market reforms, the fact remains that Egypt's private sector investment has been significantly lower than that of other developing countries. . . . Nine years after the 1991 program, private sector investment is far short of expectations, and it is hard to see a significant impact on the alleviation of poverty (Zaki, 2001)

> Private Sector Development is at the center of Egypt's economic reform program. Egypt is moving from a centrally planned, public sector dominated economy toward a competitive, market-based one in which the private sector is to play the leading role. The objective is to achieve rapid, efficient, sustainable growth, something that the past centrally planned model has not delivered. In that sense, PSD will also be crucial for the success of the country's poverty alleviation efforts.
> However, the private sector investment "response" to the reform program has been slow. While the program has brought about macroeconomic stability and has made markets more contestable, other regulatory and institutional constraints would need to be relaxed further to encourage the private sector to invest and grow efficiently (The World Bank, 1994).

What factors, according to the literature, have been responsible for impeding capitalist economic growth? Continued government intervention in the form of cumbersome bureaucracy as well as institutional constraints that raise transactions costs (Benham (1999), De Soto (2000), the World Bank (1994)), unprofitable public sector enterprises that no one wants to buy, low savings and investment rates as well as regional and political instability, have all discouraged private sector initiatives in large-scale industrialization, resulting in the failure to bring about "industrial deepening."

The issue of whether the state or the private sector should play the leading role in bringing about development has been an on-going one since the inception of modern Egypt. The project of development as embodied in the neoliberal policies of the World Bank and IMF described above, is outcomes-centered in that it is a pre-given assumption that the proliferation and predominance of private capitalist activities is a desirable *end*. To restate questions raised earlier however, is the historical experience of capitalist economic growth in the advanced industrial societies a *universal* inevitability for all societies worldwide? Is it desired by all subjects of development? Do the subjects of development in Egypt for example, desire the modernization, westernization, and individualism that accompany capitalist economic development?

STATE CAPITALISM AND UNEVEN DEVELOPMENT

As previously discussed, capitalist activities are exclusionary in that they exclude those who perform surplus labor from participating in the substantive decisions that affect their lives: they are excluded from appropriating the fruits of their labor, from having a say in how surplus labor should be distributed and from having a say in how the workplace should be organized. In advocating private capitalist practices over state-capitalist practices, neoliberal policies are merely advocating that the subjects of development in Egypt ratify the status quo such that the power to make these decisions remains within the hands of the propertied elite—who are often the very same people who make up the upper echelons of the ruling party. Advocates of neoliberal policies argue that through participation in the labor, credit and commodity markets, the benefits of capitalist economic growth will "trickle down" to the poor, the marginalized and the dispossessed. However, capitalist economic development, Marxist scholars like to point out, is never uniform or complete: rather, it is always *uneven*. Uneven capitalist development manifests itself in social contradictions such as rising disparities in the distribution of income between the rich and the poor, rising regional disparities as some parts of the country grows and others stagnate and rising sectoral disparities as some sectors of the economy flourish and others undergo crisis.

In Egypt, the effects of uneven development have manifested itself in both stark regional and sectoral disparities. Human deprivation remains severe in the South, especially in rural areas and is widespread among women. In urban Cairo, the effects of rural to urban migration have created huge disenfranchised and marginalized communities. The last two sections of this chapter examine the effects of these regional and sectoral disparities of uneven capitalist growth in Egypt.

The Geographical Dimensions of Human Deprivation in Upper Egypt

There are numerous reasons as to why the South, or the *Sa'id* or Upper Egypt as it is more commonly known, is significant for conceptualizing participatory development in Egypt. Because the Nile flows from south to north, since Pharaonic times Egypt has been divided into Upper and Lower Egypt. To this day, southern Egypt is known as "Upper" Egypt and Cairo and the northern part of the country is known as "Lower" Egypt. Modern Egypt is divided into 26 "governorates," 9 of which are south of Cairo and comprise Upper Egypt; the 9 governorates of the Nile Delta constitute Lower Egypt; there are 4 urban governorates (Cairo, Alexandria, Port Said and the Suez Canal) and 4 frontier governorates. Lower Egypt, comprising the Nile Delta region between Cairo and the Mediterranean, is the most populous region with currently about 28 million people, followed by Upper Egypt with about 24 million people. The population of Greater Cairo and the "urban governorates" of Alexandria, Port Said and the Suez is about 12 million people.[8] About 1 million people live in the "frontier" governorates of the Sinai, the Red Sea, Matrouh on the north west coast and the New Valley in the Western Desert.

Table 3.1 shows population growth rates by region. In recent years, the population of Upper Egypt has been growing at a faster pace than any other region.

Table 3.1. Regional Population Growth Rates in Egypt

Poverty by region	Annual % population growth rates		
	1960–86	1986–96	1996–2001
Urban Governorates	2.3	1.3	1.7
Lower Egypt	2.4	2.2	2
Upper Egypt	2.4	2.4	2.7
Frontier Governorates	3.8	3.8	2.6
Egypt	2.4	2.1	2.1

Source: The Egypt Human Development Report, 2003.

Despite its significance in terms of the number of people or the growth rate of the population, participation in the development process has been denied to Upper Egyptians since the inception of modern Egypt. Consequently, poverty in Upper Egypt is higher than in the other parts of the country. Ironically, Upper Egypt has been a preeminent node in the global tourism industry in since ancient times and continues to be a significant source of foreign exchange revenue. Most of the major antiquities of Ancient Egypt, such as the temples of Luxor, Karnak and Abu Simbel, the Valleys of the Queens and Kings, to name just a few are located throughout Upper Egypt. Today, the tourism sector generates the largest amount of foreign currency in the economy, exceeding the revenues from exporting petroleum products and the Suez Canal. Despite its role as a preeminent node in the global capitalist tourism industry, however, poverty and human deprivation as measured by the human development indices is more prevalent and severe in the Upper Egyptian governorates than in other parts of the country. Furthermore, recent studies suggest that poverty in the region is a "chronic" and not a temporary phenomenon (Haddad and Ahmed, 2003). The social contradictions generated by the dynamic between the deprivation of the people in the region and the presence of a lucrative tourism sector will be the subject of the case study presented in the next chapter.

Table 3.2 below shows the proportion of people below the income poverty line in Egypt. It shows that in 2004, more than every one in three Upper Egyptians live below the income poverty line. This is twice as high as the poverty rate experienced by people in the Delta region (Lower Egypt)—14%—and more than five times the rate of poverty in the urban governorates of Cairo and Alexandria (6.2%). Poverty in Upper Egypt remains significantly higher than all other regions in the country.

Table 3.2. Poverty by Region

Poverty by region (% of total Population)	Poor persons 1995/96 (%)	Poor persons 2001 (%)	Poor persons 2004 (%)
Urban Governorates	16	9	6.2
Lower Egypt	17.1	13.1	14
Upper Egypt	34.1	35.2	34
Frontier Governorates	16	10.7	n.a.
Egypt	22.9	20.1	20

Source: the Egypt Human Development Reports, 1997/98, 2003, 2005.

Between 1995 and 2004 there has barely been any change in the proportion of people in poverty. In absolute numbers the number of people in poverty in Upper Egypt has increased from 7.3 million to 8.4 million. Table 3.3 below presents a further decomposition of regional poverty by governorate. It shows that while the overall incidence of poverty in Lower Egypt decreased, the incidence of poverty in Upper Egypt as a whole has increased, with four of the eight governorates experiencing an increase in the proportion of people in poverty and four experiencing a decline. In Lower Egypt, about 3.7 million people are income-poor, with the majority of the poor in rural areas. Of the eight million people who are income- poor in Upper Egypt, about 5 million live in rural Upper Egypt. The remarkable fact to note here is that there are more than twice as many people living in poverty in Upper Egypt as there are in Lower Egypt. Moreover, there are more people in poverty in Upper Egypt today than there were in 1995/96 (*Egypt Human Development Report, 2005*).

Six kilometers north of the tourist hub of Luxor City is the governorate of Qena, once part of the same jurisdiction as Luxor. Like other Upper Egyptian Governorates, poverty in Qena is more prevalent and severe than in Egypt in general (Table 3.3 below). While Qena, like the other Upper Egyptian governorates performs worse than other parts of Egypt in terms of income poverty, even within Upper Egypt, human deprivation in Qena and Luxor take a particularly gendered aspect. Table 3.4 below provides statistics on the literacy rate, the maternal mortality rate and the infant mortality rate.

Human development indicators show that Upper Egypt also performs strikingly worse than the rest of the country in terms of the literacy rate, infant and child mortality rates, access to piped water and sanitation services (Egypt Human Development Report (EHDR), 2005). Perhaps the most glaring indicator of gender inequality in Luxor and Qena is the literacy rate. The literacy rate for women 15 years and older in Qena is the lowest in Egypt at 32%.[9] This is the lowest not only in the country, but even within Upper Egypt, where literacy rates are lower than in Egypt in general. In Cairo, by contrast 75% of women 15 and older are literate. Maternal mortality rates in Qena (per 100,000 live births) are the fourth highest in the country after Aswan, Luxor (second highest rate) and Port Said. Qena also has the lowest number of physicians per 10,000 people in the country (only 3.1) and the second lowest number of nurses per 10,000 people (4.6). Lastly, infant mortality in Qena is the highest in Upper Egypt and the second highest in the country after the frontier governorates of North Sinai.

Table 3.3. Poverty by Governorate

Governorate	Population 2001 (in thousands)	Poor persons (% of total)		No. of poor (In thousands)	
		1995/96	2001	1995/96	2001
Cairo	7,338	10.8	8.8	736	646
Alexandria	3,608	29.4	11.3	982	408
Port Said	509	3.7	2.6	17	13
Suez	457	2.4	4.2	10	19
Total	11,912	16	9	1767	1086
Lower Egypt					
Damietta	1,005	0.7	0.9	6	9
Dakhlia	4,617	11.4	17.7	482	817
Sharkiya	4,747	13.9	16.1	595	764
Kaloubiya	3,622	28.3	12.1	934	438
Kafr El Sheikh	2,426	10.1	6.7	225	163
Gharbia	3,693	9.4	10.1	320	373
Menoufia	3,025	22.8	21.7	629	656
Behera	4,384	28.5	10.4	1138	456
Ismailia	799	9.7	7.9	69	63
Total Lower Egypt	28,317	17.7	13.1	4570	3740
Urban	8,181		17.9		1464
Rural	20,137		11.3		2275
Upper Egypt					
Giza	5,662	12	18.9	574	1070
Beni Suef	2,086	34	51.2	632	1068
Fayoum	2,236	40.6	35.4	808	791
Menia	3,735	35.8	24.4	1185	911
Asyout	3,162	53.4	58.1	1496	1837
Souhag	3,526	39.4	45.5	1149	1604
Qena	2,732	38.3	33.3	935	910
Luxor	396				
Aswan	1,052	30.8	24.5	300	258
Total UE	24,187	34.1	35.2	7310	8450
Urban	7,429		36.3		2697
Rural	16,758		34.7		5815
Frontier Govs	920	16	10.7	131	98
Total Egypt	65,336			13,778	13,474

Source: Egypt Human Development Report, 2003

Table 3.4. Human Deprivation in Luxor and Qena. 2001

Governorate	Literacy 15+		Maternal Mortality rate (per 100,000 live births)	Infant Mortality rate (per 100,000 live births)
	Total	Female		
Cairo	81	75	42	38
Alexandria	80	74	59	26
Port Said	83	79	89	26
Suez	80	72	66	24
Average	81	75	89	37
Lower Egypt				
Damietta	70	67	25	18
Dakhlia	67	58	59	23
Sharkiya	62	50	53	24
Kaloubiya	69	57	30	18
Kafr El Sheikh	57	44	36	14
Gharbia	70	58	55	39
Menoufia	67	54	44	21
Behera	56	42	26	15
Ismailia	73	64	53	26
Average for Lower	65	53	23	22
Upper Egypt				
Giza	71	61	54	20
Beni Suef	51	35	49	37
Fayoum	48	34	43	34
Menia	49	33	46	42
Asyout	52	37	36	47
Souhag	50	32	51	42
Qena	50	32	86	49
Luxor	61	45	95	44
Aswan	70	58	97	25
Average for Upper	56	41	62	36

Source: Egypt Human Development Report, 2003

The female literacy rate in Qena and Luxor is low compared not only to other parts of the country (the national average is 54.2) but also to other countries such as India. It is notable that literacy rates for Qena, and indeed for most of the Upper Egyptian governorates,[10] is lower than that of not only the exemplary state of Kerala, but are also worse than the poorly per-forming Indian states such as Bihar, Punjab, Rajasthan and UttarPradesh. Hence, the remarkable point here is that not only are the levels of human deprivation high in Qena, but that in terms of women's well-being, they compare poorly with even parts of India where human development and per capita income is on the whole lower than it is in Egypt. India is an interesting country to compare with because it too suffers from uneven human development across regions (Sen and Drèze, 1999). Moreover, despite the fact that per capita income in India is about a thousand dollars less than that of Egypt, adult literacy is higher in India and has improved at a faster pace.

Table 3.5. A Comparison of Human Development Indicators Across Selected Countries

HDI Rank	Country/ State	Life Expectancy At birth 2003		Adult Literacy Rate 2003		GDP Per capita (% Age 15 and above) (PPP US$) 2003
		Female	Male	Female	Male	
119	Egypt	72.1	67.7	43.6	67.2	3,950
53	Mexico	77.5	72.6	89.5	93.4	9,168
73	Thailand	73.8	66.3	90.5	94.9	7,595
77	Philippines	72.5	68.3	92.7	92.5	4,321
94	Turkey	72.4	67.3	76.5	93.5	6,772
85	China	73.5	69.9	86.5	95.1	5,003
124	Morocco	69.5	65.8	36.1	61.8	4,004
127	India	63.8	62.8	47.8	73.4	2,892
135	Pakistan	59.8	60.2	35.2	61.7	2,097
139	Bangladesh	63.7	62.1	31.4	50.3	1,770

Source: *The Human Development Report 2005*

In fact, "The annual rate of improvement in adult literacy in Egypt (1.04%) was much lower than that of the forty developing countries" (Adams, 2000, p. 259).

Table 3.5 provides Human Development indicators for select countries in the year 2003. The Egyptian per capita income (PPP) for that year was US$ 3,635, not too far behind that of the Philippines and greater than India's per capita income (PPP) of US$2,892. The average life expectancy in Egypt is fairly close to that of someone living in Thailand, the Philippines, or Turkey, despite the fact that Egyptian per capita income is much lower. At least in terms of life expectancy Egypt has made some gains in the development process.

On the other hand, the Philippines, with only slightly higher per capita income has achieved respectable literacy rates of over 90%. The Egyptian national literacy rate of 55.6% is comparable to countries that the UNDP classifies as "least developed." It should also be noted that centrally planned economies such as China and Vietnam reported literacy rates of about 90% in 2003. The fact that a disproportionately larger amount of government expenditures is allotted to universities over primary and secondary schools have led some critics to suggest that disparities in educational attainment are due to a "striking case of class bias in education" (Richards and Waterbury, 1997, p. 119).

Sectoral imbalances and socially generated contradictions of rural-to-urban migration

In its drive to industrialize and modernize the economy, the Egyptian State has long used the agricultural sector has an instrument of its policies. Although the revolution for "Arab Socialism" did not prevent the ownership of private agricultural property, the State set up agricultural cooperatives that eventually became the sole suppliers of agricultural inputs as well as the sole buyers of agricultural output. This allowed the state to in effect tax both inputs and outputs: inputs such as fertilizers were sold at prices higher than their import prices and outputs such as cotton was bought from farmers at prices lower than the prevailing world prices. Since the 1950s the price and exchange rate structure has been used to squeeze resources out of agriculture to provide the investment needed to industrialize the economy. Aside from using the prices to extract surplus from the sector, state control over agriculture also increased to the point where the crop cycle was specified—agricultural engineers told farmers what to cultivate and this was enforced through increased policing.

The long-run effects of these policies continue to haunt policy makers today. Declining levels of private investment and hence productivity, especially in the "strategic" crops such as cotton, wheat, corn and rice. In the 1980's, this led to a fall in export earnings on the one hand and a rising import bill on the other. In time, the government had to import cereals to meet increased demand due to population growth. Eventually, as Egypt became a net importer of food, it became "hostage" to its external debtors. Low agricultural incomes have also led to an increasing migration of labor from agriculture to the domestic and foreign construction sectors.

Falling farm incomes and rising unemployment pushed farmers to migrate to urban areas in search of work; and yet the lack of steady work, low wages and a high cost of living relative to the countryside, has meant that migration to the urban areas has not brought about the sustained rise in the standard of living associated with industrialization and modernization as experienced in the West. Instead, the urban poor have turned to alternative strategies.

One course of action that became a viable option for workers in the 1970s was to emigrate to the neighboring Arab countries of Libya, Jordan, Saudi Arabia, Iraq and the Gulf states. The regional oil boom in the 1970s created a demand in these countries for unskilled and semi-skilled construction workers, drawing mostly young male workers away from farming to work abroad and thereby reducing the supply of agricultural labor in Egypt and raising agricultural wages. Richards (1994) estimated that during the oil boom, "approximately 30% of all Egyptian migrants and just under 64% of all rural migrants worked in agriculture before going abroad" (p. 250).[11]

Agricultural labor shortage during this time was further compounded by increased rural-urban migration within Egypt due to an increase in the demand for workers in the labor-intensive construction industry fueled by the influx of foreign exchange. The overall effect of both domestic and international migration was to raise real wages, consumption and the standard of living: between 1973 and 1985 real wages in farming increased by over 300%. While actual estimates of rural poverty vary,[12] there is widespread consensus that "Using any reasonable definition of poverty, Egyptian rural poverty fell sharply both absolutely and relatively during the oil boom" (Richards, 1994, p. 259).

Migration provided "unprecedented opportunities" (Amin, 1995 p. 29) for Egyptian workers, leading to a back and forth movement of people between Egypt and the neighboring Arab states, but also between rural and urban areas within the country. Traditionally, farm workers from rural farming communities migrated for work during the agricultural off-peak season and then returned to their farms when it was time to harvest (James Toth, 1999). *Sa'idi* workers from Upper Egypt in particular, have historically constituted a reserve pool of low-wage labor. The State has been able to draw upon for this mobile reserve for its numerous construction projects over the years—from the construction and yearly maintenance of the countryside's extensive system of drains and canals, to "mega" projects such as the Aswan Dam and more recently projects that involve reclaiming land from the desert. Income from migrant construction work has historically served to raise the incomes of farms in the impoverished governorates of Upper Egypt.

The oil crisis of the 70s and the consequent regional boom however, has had lasting effects on the dynamics of the labor market in Egypt. As skilled workers in the towns and cities left for better paying jobs in the neighboring oil-rich countries, workers from rural areas, especially in Upper Egypt migrated to the urban areas to take these jobs. In the 80s, as employment opportunities for Egyptian workers in the neighboring Arab countries diminished, many "repatriates bumped out their colleagues in the building trades" (Toth, 1999, p. 206). Instead of returning to their villages however, many workers from Upper Egypt remained in the cities and became part of the ranks of the unemployed and the informal sector. Rural workers from the Upper Egypt notes Toth, had "abandoned the countryside" permanently (Toth, p. 206).

The historical experience of Modernity and capitalist economic growth in the West shows that the rural-to-urban dislocation of people is often accompanied by social and cultural upheaval.

> The political problem everywhere was and remains how to manage and contain the potential explosion of masses of traumatized internal migrants living in extremely precarious conditions. They represented a frightening specter of potential political opposition to the local modernizing classes. How much better to have them leave and perhaps send back money to desperate relatives left behind! (Wolff, 2006, p 2).

This transition in Europe and North America involved societal changes from traditional to "modern" ways. Among the displaced the *sa'idi* workers in the urban areas of Cairo, however, this transition involved, not a movement to secular westernized modernity, but one that involved a return to Islamic principles. Many of the *sa'idi* workers congregated in the popular, working class *sha'abi* neighborhoods of urban Cairo.[13] These densely populated, over-crowded *sha'abi* neighborhoods provided the fertile grounds for Islamist revivalist movements.

In the 1980s, as the state began the gradual process of dismantling its social contract and cut back social expenditures on health, education, and affordable housing in urban areas, "informal" community-based institutions in these neighborhoods stepped in to fill the vacuum. Many of these informal institutions raised their funds through donations from the community at the local mosques. The funds raised through the local mosque-based charities allowed community members to decide how to distribute the money and kept the money within the immediate local economy.

> "University trained professionals who remitted their salaries home allo-
> cated a significant portion for performing Islamic good deeds, pious
> acts, and funding community development and charity projects. In the
> early 1980s such financing increased further with the profit sharing and
> monetary transactions routed through Islamic investment companies.
> Moreover, the supervision of the *zakat* funds of local private mosques
> by like-minded colleagues guaranteed that the bulk of these donations
> would reach the surrounding communities and those in need " (Toth,
> 1999, p. 211)

Beginning in 1985 however, the State began cracking down on mosques and Islamist movements throughout the country. It appointed state-sanctioned clerics to serve at the local mosques and deposited the funds raised through community-based initiatives into the government banks. The repercussions of these community-based development initiatives have had long lasting effects. A growing segment of the populace countrywide "began to realize that militancy offered the only practical way to fundamentally change the state and society" (Toth, 1999, page 216). Building on this militancy, the Muslim Brotherhood has emerged as the largest opposition movement in Egypt, winning 88 seats in the People's Assembly in 2005. In other words, the internal contradictions generated by modernity and its exclusionary development practices has, in the context of Egypt, fostered the conditions, not for secularism, but for a revival of Islamic values. The other outcome of the State's repression of community-based development initiatives has been the proliferation of informal activities, networks and associations that serve the collective interests of communities marginalized by the State.

Sectoral imbalances and socially generated contradictions of the informal sector

Once characterized as a residual phenomenon that would disappear as countries became industrialized, the informal sector[14] has taken on increased importance in the development literature on Egypt. In the year 2000, the World Bank estimated that 40% of total employment and 65% of private sector employment in Egypt was "informal." Estimates of output produced in the informal sector ranges from 30–70% of Gross Domestic Product (Galal, 2006).

The once marginalized informal sector has been generating almost 75% of new jobs in the economy in the form of small and micro-enterprises (Nassar, 2001).[15] The most recent Human Development Report on Egypt for instance, sees the sector as "a particularly attractive candidate for future employment growth" (The EHDR, 2005). Generating employment growth has become a particularly pressing issue for the State today. With more than a third of the Egyptian population consisting of people under the age of fifteen, over half a million new job seekers enter the labor market every year. Unemployment among these new labor market entrants is estimated to be at about 30%. The "modern" sector—consisting of large-scale capitalist enterprises, state-owned capitalist enterprises and the high paid, high skilled service sector jobs—has failed to generate enough employment to absorb the masses of new labor market entrants, migrants from rural areas as well as the existing unemployed (the overall official unemployment rate today is at 10%).

Not only does the informal sector provide a vehicle for relieving some of the social tension caused by a high unemployment rates, it has also been the major provider of low cost urban housing since the 1980s. On the other hand, as the magnitude of illegally constructed housing has risen, so have policy proposals that call for "formalizing the informal sector." Popularized by Hernando De Soto's provocative thesis that the "poor" in Egypt possess significant amounts of capital in the form of unlicensed shops and apartments built without the permission of the municipal authorities, the strategy to "formalize the informal sector" calls for bringing the informal "dead capital" into the circulation of "living" capital so that it can be used as collateral for loans (DeSoto, 2000). The poor in the informal economy, De Soto suggests, are really nascent capitalists, buying, selling and investing under rules and regulations other than those sanctioned by the state.

DeSoto's provocative thesis however, remains within the confines of a *capitalocentric* discourse. Can the development narrative address the informal sector without defining it in terms of its relationship to the teleology of capitalism? Can it theorize activities in the informal sector without seeing them as being traditional, marginal or nascent forms of capitalism? Can we tell the story of the informal sector in the Egyptian economy without telling it as the failure of Egypt to converge to the model of advanced industrialized capitalism? Are there anti-essentialist, anti-teleological stories of Egypt's economic development?

In the State's failed attempt to successfully formalize the informal sector, we catch a glimpse of the "lively backstage transcript of values, understandings and popular outrage" (Scott, 1997, p. 316). In Egypt, the palpable presence of the state in everyday economic practices has been countered by the rise of informal networks, associations, and institutions that clude regulation, control and co-optation by the state apparatus. While the formal institutions of participation—such as political parties, labor unions, the media and even mosques are controlled by the State—informal, community and kin-based networks are ubiquitous and go without notice. Disenfranchised by an autocratic regime and marginalized by exclusionary capitalist class processes, local communities have turned to informal institutions to create their own spaces of participation. The multitude of informal activities that now command significant economic resources in Egypt in the form of illegal real estate assets, unregistered small and microenterprises and informal savings networks offer alternative "avenues of participation" for working class neighborhoods in Cairo (Singerman, 1995; Hoodfar, 1999). Marginalized in terms of their access to the State's political apparatus, or indeed, any participation in the formal institutions dominated by the elite, these people use the "social capital" of their close-knit communities to devise economic strategies for household survival. Aside from consumption smoothing during times of economic crises, community networks are used to meet basic needs from access to housing (an extremely scarce and expensive commodity) health care, education, as well employment, credit, and community childcare services.

In this way, community and kin-based informal institutions among the residents of the popular quarters of Cairo have carved out public spaces of participation that are outside the notions of participation allowed by the discourse of Liberalism. Whereas, mainstream development notions of participation are limited to either participation through the redistributive strategies of an interventionist state or participation as access to markets, these local, community-based practices in Cairo provide indigenous Egyptian models of participation. Through their collective efforts the *sha'ab* in Cairo offer alternative perspectives on how local communities can work together towards common ends. By carving out a space between the public realm of formal politics and the private realm of individuals pursuing their self-interest, informal community networks promote voice- over the exit-oriented notions participation. Chapter Five argues that these participatory models of how *sha'abi* communities collectively condense and then redistribute their monetized wealth offer examples through which to engage alternative notions of participation, progress and development.

Chapter Four

Planning Luxor: Resistance, Contestation and Rupture in Upper Egypt

"It is a very good project to make Luxor into an international museum for everyone" (Minister of Tourism Mamdouh Al Beltagui, 1997)

"The importance of a planned and directed development cannot be overstated, because of Luxor's global significance" (The Comprehensive Development Plan for the City of Luxor, p. 9).

"There must not be a contradiction between the needs of the global economy and the welfare of our people"(President Mubarak at Davos).

Quiet deprivations are often much harder to bring to public attention than sensational events such as famine or natural disaster (Sen and Drèze, p. 264).

REPRESENTATIONAL STRUGGLES

This chapter is a close reading of both the practices and the narratives of economic development in Luxor and its adjoining governorate of Qena in Southern or "Upper" Egypt. It is on the one hand a textual deconstruction of the representations of economic development in Luxor; on the other hand, it is an unearthing of practices that have contested this narrative or continue to exist in contradiction to it. Through the representations of these practices and narratives, the area has been and continues to be the site of intensely fought struggles—both material and discursive—to lay claim to Luxor's economy and define what constitutes economic "progress" in the region.

87

Luxor City and its surrounding areas are the repository of some of the greatest remaining artistic and architectural achievements of Pharaonic Egypt. On the West Bank is the necropolis of ancient Thebes, best known for the tomb of Tutankhamun, the temple of Queen Hatshepsut as well as numerous other monuments. On the East bank are the huge temple complexes of Luxor and Karnak. Linking the two temples is the Avenue of the Sphinxes, a processional road once lined with 1,200 sphinxes. A travel destination since antiquity, Luxor today continues to be one of the most popular tourist destinations for Egypt.

Luxor has figured prominently in the Egyptian national development literature. Since the discovery of Tutankhamun's tomb in 1912, the state-run press, popular television dramas as well as official state proclamations have often been concerned with the people and the development of Luxor. Representations of Luxor have, on the one hand, taken the form of national pride in ancient Egypt's military might and architectural achievements and on the other, concern that this national heritage is threatened by human impact (Lila Abu-Lughod, 1998; Timothy Mitchell, 2002). The State has used representations of Pharaonic Egypt's imperial and military might to promote pride in a national "indigenous" Egyptian identity.[1] It has also promoted Luxor as a major site of its market-oriented economic policies: an export-oriented development strategy based on the export of tourism services. "It is a very good project" the Minister of Tourism, Mamdouh Al Beltagui has declared, "to make Luxor into an international museum for everyone" (Larter, 1997). Accordingly, the latest incarnation of government plans[2] for developing Luxor City has been to liberalize labor laws, privatize state-owned hotels and offer tax exemptions to attract multinational firms in the tourism industry (much like the conditions created in export processing zones to attract multinational firms in the textiles and garments industries).

While representations of Luxor as a preeminent node in global flows of tourism and foreign exchange dominate the development literature, there are however, other representations of Luxor, ones that for example describe the local communities of Luxor. Unlike Luxor-the-place, representations of Luxor-the-community argue that the people have not been conducive to the Government's strategy of economic development. The people of the region—Upper Egypt and Upper Egyptians in general—are frequently the object of representations in popular culture, the media and everyday usage. Compared to "modernized," urbanized Cairenes, Upper Egyptians, or *Sai'idis*, have been for years portrayed as being illiterate, impoverished, and stuck in rural backwardness (Lila Abu-Lughod, 1998). Stereotypes of *Sai'idis* in the vernacular, television dramas and other national media depict them as being darker-skinned, less intelligent and prone to religiously moti-vated violence (Mitchell, 1991, 2002).[3]

Representations of the communities in Luxor in particular are concerned about the impact of human settlements on the area's monuments. Over the course of centuries, settlements, buildings and roads have grown up, around and on top of many of the ancient ruins. The City has also encroached on the Luxor temple: a mosque sits atop ruins within the confines of the temple complex. Settlements have also grown up and around the ruins on the West bank. The Colossi of Memnii sit among cultivated fields of *berseem*[4] [figure 2] and the entire village of Gurna is built of mud brick homes that sit among and on top of the tombs of Pharaonic nobles [figure 3]. Concern for the pres-ervation of these tombs is reflected in the State's development policies, which have repeatedly tried to remove and relocate local residents away from the vicinity of the tombs and temples to state-planned housing.

Over the years however, local communities have resisted relocation and contested their rights to have access to the area's monuments. These acts of resistance have been represented as being against the national inter-est of economic development and modernization by the popular press and media. When the communities refused to relocate they were "accused of destroying the archaeological sites that are not part of the wider national heritage but world heritage" (Abu-Lughod, p. 162, 1998) and were remon-strated for being against national goals of progress and development.

This chapter unpacks these multiple representations of Luxor and its communities and argues that these discourses embody *material* struggles to define and lay claim to Luxor's economy. I suggest that in the context of Luxor, the discourse of development planning situated as it is in ideas of nationalism and cultural heritage, is, in the name of capitalist economic growth, effectively redistributing customary property rights away from local communities to multinational firms associated with the global tour-ism industry. In other words, in the language of class analysis, through the discourse of nationalism and modernity and its accompanying practices of economic development, the state is in effect securing the conditions of exis-tence for the prevalence of capitalist class processes in Luxor.

Furthermore, this chapter will show that the continued human depri-vation in the area is the outcome of the exclusionary nature of development policies that favor capitalist labor practices. This chapter, therefore, sub-stantiates my earlier argument that despite the rhetoric of "participatory development" in the mainstream literature, the principal conceptualizations of participation in economic development remain partial and inadequate.

The trajectory of this chapter is as follows: the first section discusses the dominant representations of Luxor in the literature on economic development.

As a locality that generates significant flows of foreign exchange, Luxor represents a nationally and internationally significant node in the flows of foreign capital and, as such, it has figured prominently in the Egyptian national development literature. Paradoxically, despite the region's lucrative tourist industry, the City and the district of Luxor are surrounded by one of the most impoverished governorates in the country and have been the sites of numerous development "missions"—missions carried out by the national state, the World Bank, the United Nations Development Programme (UNDP) and numerous non-government development organizations. This section draws on the representations of Luxor in the project documents of the World Bank and the government of Egypt. The second section revisits the human deprivation in Luxor and Upper Egypt in general. In privileging Luxor's significance as a site of transnational flows of investment capital, the dominant narrative of economic development suppresses the human deprivation of the region.

The third section explores alternative ways to think and practice development by using class analysis to de-center capitalism and construct an alternative representation of economic activity in Luxor and its surrounding areas. The last section of the chapter deconstructs the familiar representation of Luxor's capitalist enclaves of walled and gated tourist resorts and show how local communities have contested the exclusionary nature of development practices through everyday acts of resistance. Other than being represented as a source of national pride and national wealth, Luxor has also figured prominently in the national and international media as a site of recurring violence against Western tourists. While the dominant narrative of development depicts these incidents of violence as marginal and "religiously motivated," to what extent are these acts of resistance grounded in the severity of human deprivation in the region? To what extent do these acts of contestation embody the off-stage discourse—or what James Scott calls "the hidden transcripts"—of dispossessed local communities that have been marginalized by the uneven and exclusionary effects of capitalist development practices?

Luxor's place in the dominant narrative of globalization and economic development

A tourist destination since antiquity, Luxor today continues to be one of the most lucrative tourist destinations in the country, replete with luxury hotels, resorts and cruise ship lines, generating significant flows of foreign exchange. In 1999 the UNDP estimated that tourism in Luxor generated about US$420 millionper year in foreign exchange revenues.[5] Hence, as a significant source of foreign exchange, Luxor is vital to the State's export-led strategy of economic development. This strategy is the cornerstone of the dominant narrative of globalization and development in economics and is operationalized through a set of policies referred to as structural adjustment and stabilization. In this narrative global markets are represented as conduits of wealth. By "opening" themselves to global financial and commodity markets, local economies are able to enter and partake in the global generation of wealth.

The putative telos in this narrative is that by "opening" the local economy to globalized forces such as transnational companies that will invest in the tourism industry, Luxor will be able to increase the quality and quantity of its exports of tourism services (hotels, airfare, tour packages etc). These exports will generate foreign exchange revenues, jobs and thereby increase social well-being. Much of this strategy is embodied in "*The Comprehensive Development Plan for the City of Luxor*" (henceforth CDCL)[6]—the State's economic plan for developing the area. As the main project document summarizing the State's development strategy, the CDCL states early on that, "The importance of a planned and directed development cannot be overstated, because of Luxor's global significance" (The Comprehensive Development Plan for the City of Luxor, p. 9). Indeed, in recognition of its significance as a site that generates considerable flows of foreign exchange, the State has granted the city of Luxor its own jurisdiction status as an area that has evolved into a "tourism-processing zone."

Embodied in the CDCL is a plan to transform Luxor into an "Open Air Museum, an export processing zone that exports mass produced "tourism packages" for the public "consumption of ancient Egypt" (Mitchell, 2002). The CDCL is a bold and ambitious plan expected to take up to twenty years to complete. It has three major objectives. First and foremost, the CDCL's objective is to maximize revenue from tourism. In order to fulfill this objective, it calls for investment in a) renovating and excavating existing monuments and b) in building a new tourist resort village to encourage tourists to lengthen their stay. Plans for the tourist village—El Toud—envisions 18 new four and five star hotels consisting of 4, 500 rooms, as well as a golf course, tennis courts, a museum, a theatre, gardens and a raised causeway connecting the resort to a cruise ship port on the Nile.

The CDCL's second objective is to "alleviate population pressure and its impact on the city's antiquities."[7] The current population of Luxor City and Luxor Markaz is estimated to be about 400,000 people. About 161, 500 people live in Luxor city, while the rest live in the surrounding Luxor Markaz. The population is projected to grow to about 1 million people by 2017. In Luxor City alone, tourist visitors are expected to increase from slightly over a million today to about 4 million in 2017. This projected increase in both the local population as well as the number of visitors every year is the main impetus behind formulating urban plans for the city of Luxor.

The CDCL hopes to alleviate population pressure by creating a "planned community" New Luxor, south of the present city for a target population of 200,000 residents. As part of this objective, about one hundred homes currently located on top of the Avenue of the Sphinxes are to be demolished and their residents relocated. Furthermore, construction of buildings in Luxor, both on the East and West banks are to be severely restricted.

Third the CDCL plans to "create economic opportunities for the citizens of the region" through the "introduction of and support for the cultivation of higher-value crops in the agricultural zone surrounding the City of Luxor" (CDCL, *Project Summary* September 6, 1999, Luxor, Egypt).

The UNDP's Interventions to include the local community in the Comprehensive Development Plans for Luxor

From the beginning of its involvement in the planning process, the United Nations' Development Programme (UNDP) was concerned that the plan as it stood was geared towards attracting large private capitalist firms to invest in large-scale tourism projects and did not address the needs of the local communities or involve their participation.[8] In keeping with the World Bank's structural adjustment packages of the 1980s and 1990s, the CDCL's vision of development was oriented towards attracting "private sector investment": most of the development funds forthcoming from the state and international donors would be awarded to large private construction companies and international hotel management firms.

Moreover, during the structural adjustment and liberalization period in the late 1980s and early 1990s, in accordance with the Government of Egypt's move towards a market-oriented economy, many of Luxor's state-owned assets had already been privatized and sold to foreign multinational firms on generous terms. As with export-processing zones worldwide, the Government of Egypt had also accorded Luxor special jurisdiction status, independent of its encircling governorate, Qena (see map), so that investors could enjoy competitive labor costs, "outstanding profits in the tourism field" and face no restrictions on the repatriation of those profits.[9]

Thus, given that the State's role in the appropriation and distribution of wealth generated by tourism has diminished, the UNDP's objective was to ensure that there were provisions within the CDCL that allowed the local communities to benefit from this strategy of economic development.[10] In other words, from the early stages of its involvement with the CDCL planning process, the UNDP was concerned about the mechanism through which the local communities of Luxor would be able to partake of the wealth generated by the tourism and tourism related industries promoted by the State and World Bank.

The project document—the CDCL—acknowledged "There is substan tial poverty in Luxor, despite the appearance of wealth because of the tourism industry" (p. 16). Its policies that addressed the well-being of the local communities involved the introduction of high value agriculture to the area. The CDCL plans called for cultivating highly perishable fruits and vegetables such as grapes, strawberries, melons, tomatoes and string beans, establishing agro-processing plants to process and package them, and then exporting them to national and international urban areas. The UNDP was concerned therefore that the CDCL plans were excluding the local communities from the employment opportunities in the tourism, construction and tourism related service and manufacturing industries. Thus, one of the main objectives of the UNDP's intervention was to investigate the channels through which the local labor force could have access to jobs in the construction and tourism sectors and thus "participate" in the employment and income-generating opportunities offered by Luxor's global tourist industry.[11]

Clearly, the meaning of "participation" in the UNDP's narrative is limited in practice to *participation in markets*—in this case mainly the labor market. According to the export-led strategy of development, in return for the special rights and privileges accorded by the state, the tourism resorts would not only bring in foreign exchange revenue, but they would hire local workers. In this strategy, the labor market is the implicit conduit through which the wealth generated by the tourism industry is to "trickle-down" to the people of the area. Increased investment in tourism infrastructure would accommodate the expected increase in the number of tourists (4 million by 2017) and hence generate a higher demand for workers in tourism related industries, as well as demand for local agricultural goods and manufactured goods produced by the local small businesses. For the local community, therefore these tourism "enclaves" would generate jobs, income and hence social well-being.

A narrative that is suppressed by the dominant discourse of an export-led strategy of economic development is that despite more than a century of foreign investment in tourism in the area,[12] the wealth generated by the tourism industry had done little to improve the standard of living of the surrounding communities. Moreover, levels of human deprivation in Luxor and its surrounding communities remain among the highest in the nation. In reality the much-coveted jobs in the tourism industry have historically remained out of the local communities' reach, most of whom, not only do not possess the type of skills that would make them attractive to potential employers in the tourism industry, but are unable even to read and write. In the following section I discuss the lack of human development in the area.

Luxor and its surrounding communities as sites of human deprivation

The UNDP's concern to include the excluded was particularly pressing given that although the region generates millions of dollars in foreign exchange revenue, it nevertheless suffers from levels of human deprivation that are among the highest in the country. As discussed in Chapter Three, Upper Egypt has suffered through decades of persistent and chronic poverty and educational attainment levels that are lower than the rest of the country. To what extent therefore, are the subjects of development participating in these economic practices that generate huge global flows of wealth through tourism? Why have human development indicators in Qena remained as low as they are, given the area's proximity to one of Egypt's most lucrative tourist areas? Why are Luxor and Qena so poor despite centuries of access to global capital flows? What role has development "planning" played in excluding local communities in the vicinity of Luxor?[13]

The narrative of economic development has narrowly defined what constitutes economic progress in the region. The emphasis in particular has been on the strategy of "development as export-led economic growth," a strategy that fosters capitalist activities as the only viable path to progress. In this narrative of what constitutes "development" local communities have no alternative but to endure the hardships in the short run, restructure their economies and hope to produce globally competitive goods in the long run.[14] Capital accumulation through export-led industrialization and economic growth is presented the single path to prosperity and hence.[15]

In being party to this strategy and despite all intentions, the UNDP's narrative of "including the excluded" remains within the confines of an outcomes-centered view of development. Participation in this narrative is limited to exploitative wage-labor jobs in the capitalist activities of Luxor's tourism resorts. Within mainstream neoclassical economics, a worker's right to a share of an economy's resources is contingent on his or her ability to access markets—mainly the market for labor, followed by the credit market, the land market etc. Consequently, when the discourse of economic development on Luxor addresses local community participation in the distribution of economic resources, it does so from the perspective of participation in markets: the labor market for tourism-related industries, the construction industry and the markets for high value agricultural products.

This narrative of development in the region suggests that local communities have to "jump on the bandwagon" of globalized capitalist practices or else be left behind." It does not question the inadequacy of this sort of limited participation in the development process. The conceptual poverty of what constitutes participation in this context is disempowering: it de-politicizes participatory development initiatives at the community level, and down-plays the ability of communities to voice their own notions of progress and development.

As argued in Chapters One and Three the principles of the market-place are inimical to substantive notions of participation. An understanding of participation based on the ethos of markets is "exit" based: if you wish to participate in the development process you get a job in a tourist resort—if not, you exit from the tourism labor market. This tendency to prefer exit to voice as a strategy promotes a poor notion of participation and denies communities the right to voice their ideas of how to organize activities in the tourism sector. The undue emphasis on the aesthetics of markets system as an allocative mechanism is not appropriate to allocate participation in the development process.

Nor should capitalist activities be conflated with market activities as they often are in the development literature. Capitalism is often equated with the distributive mechanism of the market, both within and outside the economics discipline. Phrases such as "market reforms," "market liberaliza-tion" and "a free market economy" used in the context of policies pursued by the World Bank and the International Monetary Fund often constitute representations of "capitalism." Not all that is bought and sold in a market however, is produced under a *capitalist class process*; and goods produced under *non-capitalist class processes* can also benefit from the efficient alloca-tive attributes of market exchange. For example, worker collectives, as well as independent self-proprietors, may also sell their wares in markets, though these commodities were not produced under capitalist class processes. Let me explain what postmodern Marxists understand by "class process," and in particular, what they mean by the capitalist class process.

Dominant narratives of the economy conflate the market exchange of commodities with capitalism. Marxian theory however, makes this distinction clear: the market exchange of commodities does not constitute capitalism. While capitalism is a *class process*, the market exchange of commodities is considered to be a *non-class process* in the Marxian theoretical framework. The concept of class as a process involves the performance, appropriation and distribution of *surplus labor*. A capitalist class process is one in which workers participate in the performance of *surplus labor* but are excluded from appropriating the *surplus value* that they create. Surplus labor arises from the fact that each worker in a capitalist enterprise produces enough wealth in a workday to sustain her or himself (for which the worker is compensated in wages) and also a surplus that is appropriated by the capitalist. As Resnick and Wolff have pointed out however, non-Marxian narratives of the economy are silent about the concepts of surplus labor and "class as process" (1994, p. 89). The capitalist class process therefore, is exclusionary because it denies workers the right to participate in the appropriation and distribution of surplus labor! Being excluded from the appropriative and distributive moments constitutes *exploitation* in a Marxian sense. Dominant narratives of economic activity however, suppress the notion of exploitation by denying the existence of this "invisible flow of labor" (Resnick, Wolff, Gibson-Graham, 2000 p. 4) from the worker to the capitalist.

As a consequence of this conflation between capitalism and market exchange dominant narratives of economic activity occlude the postmodern Marxist preference for non-exploitative, participatory ways of organizing economic activities that may also be "market-oriented." For instance, worker collectives such as the Mondragon cooperatives in the Basque country sell their output in various markets but collectively appropriate their surplus labor (Ellerman, 1990, Gibson-Graham, 2003). In these collectives, output is distributed in commodity form, workers work for wages but participate in the appropriation of their surplus labor. Similarly self-employed entrepreneurs, who single-handedly produce and appropriate their own surplus labor, may sell their output in a market but would not be considered capitalists. A "market oriented enterprise" need not be exclusionary at the moment of surplus appropriation. By acknowledging the existence of surplus labor and by accounting for the various ways in which surplus labor is performed, appropriated and distributed, postmodern Marxists avoid the conflation between market activity and capitalism.

A class analytic approach to economic participation thus provides a theoretical framework for conceptualizing worker participation in not only producing surplus labor, but also participation in appropriating and distributing it (Cullenberg (1992, 1998) and Chakrabarti and Cullenberg (2001 and 2003)). There are therefore, three moments of participation to consider, participation in the production of surplus labor, in the appropriation of surplus labor and in its distribution.[16] This is a much more complete notion of economic participation than the dominant notion of participation in the dominant development literature, which only addresses participation in the production of surplus labor (through the ability to perform in the labor market for instance) but not the appropriative and distributive moments. In other words, the postmodern Marxist theory of economic participation, organized as it is around the notion of surplus labor, explicitly addresses distributive economic justice such that workers are involved, not just in the generation of surplus, but also in deciding who will appropriate surplus and how it will be distributed.[17] In other words, if members of a community can be justified in claiming participation in political processes, in shop-floor organizational issues at the workplace, in the allocation of resources at home and in the larger society, then why not in the participation of the fruits of their labor?[18]

Analyzing the extent and ways in which producers of surplus labor participate in the appropriation and distribution of surplus labor—a "labor theory of participation"—provides a voice-based notion of participatory development as opposed an "exit" based conceptualization of participation. This labor theory of participation however, has been absent in the mainstream conceptualization of participatory development.

How then can we think and practice development differently? How can we theorize non-capitalist activities without seeing them as being traditional, marginal or nascent forms of capitalism? How can we tell a story of Luxor's economy without it being the story of capitalism in the region? How can we engage local voices in this discussion? In spite of all intentions to engage the local communities through the techniques of "participatory research," the UNDP's Human Development paradigm remains within a capitalist ontology: it does not have the framework to enable it to tap into the radical possibilities embodied in the heterogeneity of economic practices in Luxor. In practice capitalist activities retain their centrality in the UNDP's plans for development in the region. Luxor's economic terrain however, consists of a diversity culturally specific ways of organizing economic activity, some of which involve participatory labor practices. These diverse, non-capitalist ways of organizing economic activities, however, are "invisible" or marginalized in the dominant narratives of export-led economic development. The first step in thinking differently about development involves therefore, the ontological move to "de-center capitalism."

De-centering capitalism in Luxor:

Gibson-Graham and Ruccio (2001) suggest that there are three ways to de-centering capitalism: one way is to deconstruct familiar representations of the economy, a second way is to produce different representations of economic activity and a third way is to develop different narratives of economic development. By categorizing the diverse ways in which surplus labor is produced, appropriated and distributed in any given economic landscape, the class analytical framework provides alternative representations of economic activity, based on the three moments of participation—participation in the performance, appropriation and distribution of labor.

Table 4.1 below provides an alternative representation of Luxor's economy. It shows that wage labor, the market exchange of commodities and capitalist enterprise exist among a diversity of ways by which communities in Luxor produce, exchange and distribute values.

Table 4.1. The Class Diversity of Luxor's Economy

Organizational form	Output Distribution	Worker remuneration	Surplus
Independent Class Process Independent small scale producers at the local bazaar, restaurants, taxi drivers, local tour guides, mini-bus operators, craft producers, sail boat owners, ferry boat owners, barbers, women headed households	Distributed in commodity form in the local markets	Money or in-kind	Individuals who perform, appropriate and distribute their own surplus.
Capitalist Class Process Manufactured goods and high-end services (tourism enclaves) • Hotels • Restaurants • Tours • Cruise ships About 5% of farms in the region are capitalist	**Commodity** Global and national tourism markets-Output is distributed in commodity form	**Wage-labor** • Hotel employees • Cruise ship employees • Tour operators	Workers perform surplus but are excluded from appropriating it.
State Capitalist • State-run monuments • Sugar-cane processing factory (state-owned enterprises)	**Commodity** The "consumption of ancient Egypt": over the years the State has commodified Luxor's archaeological sites **Non-commodity** Some sugar is distributed as a state-subsidized commodity	**Non-wage** Government employees who are paid wages	Workers perform surplus but are excluded from appropriating it. State-appointed board of directors appropriate and distribute surplus
Feudal class process • Small farms that grow wheat, maize, vegetables, onions, • Growing berseem for fodder • Patriarchal Households • Bread-making	**Non-commodity**— most of the output is produced for the purposes of self-provisioning	**Non-wage** Feudal farmers	Family members participate in the production of SL but "patriarch" appropriates and distributes it

(continued)

Table 4.1. The Class Diversity of Luxor's Economy (continued)

Organizational form	Output Distribution	Worker remuneration	Surplus
Communal Class processes • Vegetables, onions, mulukhiyya, maize • Raising water buffalos, cows, goat and sheep • Sugar-cane is cut and stripped by family members with the help of friends and relative s	Non-commodity Self-provisioning for household consumption **Commodity** Sugar-cane is sold to the state in commodity form	Non-wage Animal husbandry work on family farms is mostly done by women only Crops for household consumption are raised and harvested by hand by family members	Shared distribution of surplus among family and community members (depending on the output)

In Luxor, the most visible capitalist activities are the "tourism processing zones"—large multinational firms that employ waged labor in the resorts with their hotels, shops and restaurants, the luxury cruise ships on the Nile, the airlines and the international tour agencies that market and sell tour packages abroad. In this exploitative way of organizing economic activity workers are excluded from the appropriation of their surplus labor.

The feudal, independent and communal tiers may be invisible in the dominant narratives of economic development, but class analysis reveals that Luxor's economic landscape is rife with these diverse practices. In other words, although dominant economic representations are fixated on capitalist activities, capitalist class structures coexist among a heterogeneity of ways to organize the production, appropriation and distribution of surplus labor.

The data in table 4.2 below is drawn from the Egypt Labor Market Survey (1998). The survey categorizes workers by waged worker, employer, self-employed and non-waged householder. The table illustrates the fact that *at least* 54% of the rural population in Upper Egypt is primarily engaged in non-capitalist activities—non-waged household workers and self-employed workers. The non-waged household worker and self-employed worker categories broadly cover the independent, feudal and communal class processes.

Moreover, of the remaining 46% of the population, studies of agricultural practices in rural areas and in Qena in particular, reveal that "waged workers" and "employers" are simultaneously involved in numerous economic activities, holding multiple class positions, some of which may be communal class processes. For example, men who for work wages for large farmers in the area (capitalist class position) also cultivate their own smaller plots for household consumption. Family members cultivate wheat, rice and vegetables together and the surplus from these activities is collectively produced, appropriated and distributed constituting a communal class process. Even the large farmers who may hold capitalist class positions appropriating and distributing the surplus labor produced by their hired workers, may also hold the position of the patriarchal feudal "lord" when they appropriate and distribute the surplus labor produced by the women in their household. Attention to the myriad of ways in which surplus labor is produced, appropriated and distributed provides insight into the diversity and complexity of Luxor and Qena's economy.

Table 4.2. Employment in Upper Egypt by Work Status

Employment in rural Upper Egypt by work status	Workers	As a % of
Category	(In thousands)	The rural UE pop.
Waged Worker		
Male	1,895	61.0
Female	189	7.0
Total	2,084	36
Employer		
Male	546	17.6
Female	24	0.9
Total	570	9.8
Self-employed		
Male	292	9.4
Female	84	3.1
Total	376	6.47
Non-waged Household worker		
Male	372	12.0
Female	2,412	89.0
Total	2,784	48
Total Male pop	3,105	
Total female pop	2,709	
Total Upper Egypt rural pop.	5,814	100

Source: Table 15-A Egypt Labor Market Survey 1998

Enterprises as the sites of surplus production

There are three sites of surplus production, appropriation and distribution that postmodern Marxists typically use as the context for class analysis (Resnick and Wolff, 1994; Chakrabarti and Cullenberg, 2001, 2003). They are the private enterprise, the state enterprise and the household. In Luxor—as in rural areas of other developing countries—the household is also where enterprise activity takes place.

In Luxor, much of local non-farm economic activity takes the form of independent small-scale producers (small businesses) at the local *bazaars:* artisans, barber shops, restaurants, taxi drivers, mini-bus operators (an inexpensive form of transportation used by the local community), as well as ferry and sailboat owners. Some produce wares for the local market (pottery, glass, rugs, textiles, alabaster statues, papyrus etc), some sell their services as market commodities (such as haircuts, ferry rides, sailboat and taxicab rides to tourists). These enterprises consist of a single individual who perform, appropriate and distribute their own surplus and thus constitute the *independent* class processes. Based on the categories used by the labor market survey (Table 4.2), almost 10% of the male population cited self-employment as their main job. Various agricultural activities on small family farms may also take the form of the *independent* class process.

Table 4.3. Men and Women's Main Sector of Economic Activity in Upper Egypt

Employed Men by Main Economic Activity (thousands)		As % of rural pop.	Employed Women by Main Economic Activity (thousands)		As % of rural pop.
Agriculture	1276	41.1	Agriculture	2402	89
Services	612	19.7	Services	106	4
Trade	333	10.7	Trade	148	5
Manufacturing	335	10.8	Manufacturing	41	2
Construction	348	11.2	Construction	5	0
Transport	149	4.8	Transport	3	0
Other	52	1.7	Other	4	0
Total	3105	100.0	Total	2709	100

Source: Table 14 AR Egypt Labor Market Survey 1998

The farm-household enterprise as a site of surplus production

Table 4.3 shows that 89% of women and 41% of men in rural Upper Egypt report agriculture as their main economic activity. Decomposing labor market data by gender, (Assad, 1998) finds that while there has been an absolute decrease in the number of men working in agriculture, there has been a significant increase in women working in agriculture. Women outnumber men as agricultural workers in every age bracket of the ELMS: a phenomenon referred to as "the feminization" of Egyptian agriculture (Assad, 1998).

As discussed in the preceding chapter, men in Upper Egypt have traditionally supplemented income from family farms by taking on jobs in sectors like construction, during the agricultural off-peak season. During peak season when, farms need extra workers, men return to the agricultural sector (Toth, 1999). Toth's account Upper Egypt suggests that although men may not cite farming as their "main" economic activity, farming labor practices still dominates the life of local communities in places like Qena. The seasonal nature of agriculture as well as the gendered division of tasks on farms, involves men employed in non-farm activities returning to the farm during the particular months of the year when specific crops are to be sown and harvested. For instance, sowing maize and harvesting wheat have traditionally been regarded as "men's work." Conversely, cattle and poultry husbandry is regarded as "women's work." [19]

In general, labor practices vary by the type of crop that is cultivated (Hopkins, 1999; Mitchell, 2002, Toth, 1999) and play a significant role in determining the class processes that occur on a farm-household-enterprise. Small family farms are sites where numerous class processes take place, with men and women holding multiple class positions. In other words alongside factors such as the size of a farm and the laws determining property ownership, traditional *labor practices* are likely to affect the types of class processes that occur on farm household enterprises in Luxor and Qena. Let me explain what I mean by looking at the labor practices involved in the cultivation of particular crops in the region.

Power, Property and Class

The vast majority of farms in the region (and in Egypt as a whole) are "small farms": studies of land distribution show that 90% of farmers have access to less than 5 feddans (about 5.19 acres) of land (Bush, 1998). According to official government statistics the average plot size is 1.84 feddans (almost 2 acres), but often plots are smaller due to a high degree of fragmentation.[20] Thus large-scale, mechanized, cultivation associated with capitalist farms in the United States and Europe is not prevalent in the Egyptian country-side. In fact farming in Egypt remains relatively less capital intensive than in other parts of the world.

Privately owned land is the most common type of landholding and these small family farms produce mainly for household consumption pur-poses. Numerous studies find that the bulk of production on small family farms is carried out for household consumption and not to sell for cash in the market. For example, 70% of farmers who grew wheat, and 80% of those who grew maize, grew it for their own household consumption (Nassar, Sands, Omran and Krenz, 1996; Mehanna, Hopkins and Abdel-maksoud, 1994). Half of the berseem crop, the clover used as fodder in Egypt, is used for feeding the household cattle and the rest sold to other households in the village. In his study of Qena, Mitchell finds that "crops intended for the farm household now account for more than two-thirds of the crop area" (1998, p. 34).

As already established, farming is the dominant way of life in the region, with almost all women and (at least) 41% of men citing agriculture as their main economic activity (ELMS, 1998). Since the bulk of produc-tion on these small family farms is for household consumption that means the output is distributed in *non-commodity form*. Furthermore, since these farms are owned and operated by the family, family members are paid in *non-wage* form. Distributing output in non-commodity form, and compen-sating workers in non-wage form is common to all class processes except capitalism. In other words, non-capitalist class processes are widely preva-lent among household farm-enterprises in the region. Unpacking the ways in which workers are remunerated (wage/non-wage), output is distributed (market/non-market), as well as the extent to which workers are included from appropriating and distributing surplus labor, reveals the heterogene-ity of Luxor's economy. Not only are capitalist activities displaced from the central position they hold in the official development narrative of the CDCL, but class analysis also allows us to see the ways in which local eco-nomic activities are embedded in multiple social, cultural, political, envi-ronmental processes. For instance, the social construction of gender in the region and the prevailing system of patriarchal authority[21] governs the rela-tions of power between men, women and children, determines the gender division of labor and hence influences the extent to which women partici-pate in the decision affecting the distribution of surplus labor.

Work on small family farms is usually divided along traditional gen-der lines, with women being responsible for animal husbandry (raising water buffalos, goats and chicken), dairy production, as well as vegetable cultivation (Hopkins, 1999; Toth, 1999). Men are expected to perform the more physically demanding tasks such as plowing, harrowing, irrigation etc (Toth, 1999). However, as Toth notes, "women are not merely relegated to housework and animal husbandry alone. They also work in the fields alongside men, cultivating crops such as wheat, cotton, corn, clover and rice" (ibid, p. 63). His study provides crucial insight into the *nonclass processes* of patriarchy and the social construction of gender in the region. He notes that the "boundary between men's and women's work is not a physiological certainty. Instead it is a cultural misrepresentation since despite the belief in innate gender differences, it is repeatedly crossed by both male and female workers" (ibid, p.63). Hence, studies such as those by Toth, Hopkins and Mitchell show that though there are prevailing notions of what constitutes "women's work" and "men's work," when the need arises (such as during harvesting season) men and women cross the gender boundary to ensure the successful cultivation of crops.

Animal husbandry and dairy production for example, are tasks allocated to women by the gendered division of labor. Where an individual performs, appropriates and distributes her own surplus labor, she is involved in an *independent* class process. Output from an independent class process may be distributed in noncommodity form—such as, for example, a woman who cultivates *berseem* (a plant used as fodder for cattle) on a family owned plot to feed to her goats is involved in producing, appropriating and distributing her own surplus labor. Alternatively, she may make goat cheese, sell it to her neighbors and then use the money to buy clothes for herself and her family. In this case the output from her activity is distributed in commodity form. The independent class structure could constitute both these activities, with the only distinction that in the first case output is distributed in noncommodity form, while in the second case output is distributed in commodity form. Nonclass religious and cultural processes create the conditions of existence for women's independent class structures: because Islamic law states that women are entitled to their own wealth, in general women retain control over their earnings, and social mores impugn men who make claims over their wife's earnings.

The cultivation of cotton, wheat, and maize involve both male and female family members working together (Toth, 1999). Wheat and maize are most commonly produced for household consumption. Communal class processes therefore constitute these activities: workers are remunerated in nonwage form, output is distributed in noncommodity form and family members collectively perform, appropriate and distribute their surplus labor. Cotton cultivation takes a particular communal form. Cotton is a crop that has been historically regulated by the government. In the past, farmers were given quotas to fulfill and their output would be sold to the State. It is therefore, distributed in commodity form (although markets are heavily regulated). Hence, men and women collectively perform and appropriate the surplus labor involved in the cultivation of cotton, but given that men are the ones involved in transporting cotton to the State's procurement offices, they may be the ones who decide how the cash (or surplus value) from selling cotton is distributed. In this case, communal class processes most likely take a particular form: that of a *patriarchal communal class structure*.[22] This form of communal class process depends on a patriarchalsystem of power where the head of the household is the father/ husband/ grandfather/ uncle/ brother etc. Under patriarchal communal class processes, surplus labor is produced and appropriated collectively but distribution decisions are made either by the male head alone or in consultation with other male members of the household. In class terms under the patriarchal communal class structure the performative and appropriative moments involve participatory practices, while the patriarch controls the distributive moment, or subsumed class process. Toth's study of Upper Egyptian society suggests that it is more patriarchal than other parts of the country (ibid, p. 63). However, anthropological studies document instances of Egyptian women appealing to the religious and cultural preeminence accorded to the re-production of the family to assert their entitlement to the family's pool of surplus (Hoodfar, 1999 and Singerman, 1997). Further research is needed to better understand the intersections of gender, patriarchy and power over the distributive moment of surplus labor.

Although this may be the most common form of communal class process occurring in rural households, there may be other class processes existing and arising. Along with the phenomenon of the feminization of agriculture, the 1995/1996 Egypt Household Income/Expenditure Survey (EHIES) notes that of the 711 households in the Qena governorate 139 are female-headed households. Thus the predominance of women in agricultural activities as well as the rising incidence of female-headed households may well be affecting the ownership patterns, power structures and class processes of these households. The absence of male authority may result in the failure to reproduce nonclass processes such as notions of patriarchal power and the traditional social construction of gender. Since these nonclass processes made up the conditions of existence for the previous class structures of these household farm-enterprises, the old class structures may change. The consequent new relations of power and patterns of property ownership are likely to affect the way surplus labor is produced, appropriated and distributed in these female-headed households, and perhaps bring into existence alternative, yet-to-be-conceptualized class processes. The ways in which in power relations, gender norms and property ownership

articulate with various class processes in female-headed households promises to be an interesting direction for future research.

Along with wheat, maize, berseem, onions and vegetables for household consumption, almost all farms in the region maintain a small field of
sugarcane. In terms of the area cultivated, sugarcane is the dominant crop
in Luxor (table 4.4). Sugarcane is cut and stripped by the men in the family
with help of extended family members and their friends. In class terms, this
means that sugarcane is a crop that is cultivated on family-owned property
and harvested using collective labor practices. The harvest is then sold to
the state-run sugar factories[23] and the surplus value from the sale of sugarcane is communally appropriated. The communal class process constituting
the cultivation and harvesting of sugar cane on small and medium farms
may also be patriarchal in nature, with surplus labor being performed,
appropriated and by the male members of households, and the elder men
controlling the distributive moment.

The communal class process involved in harvesting sugarcane may take
a hitherto unspecified form: the labor power involved in harvesting sugarcane
is exchanged in reciprocal fashion among members of a village. The specifics
of this collective performance of surplus labor most likely affects the way in
which community members appropriate and distribute surplus value from the
sale of the cane. Moreover, it is interesting to note that the organization of
region's market[24] or "cash crop" emerges as a site of *collective* labor practices.
Thus sugarcane illustrates my point from earlier in this chapter that market
activities are not synonymous with capitalist activities, and that market activities need not be exclusionary at the moment of surplus appropriation.

Table 4.4. Major Crops Cultivated in the District of Luxor (1 feddan = 1.038 acres)

Crop	Feddans
Sugarcane	22,447
Wheat	13,934
Beans	1,250
Lentils	93
Vegetables	780
Garlic	19
Shair	5
Other	2,982
Total area used for horticultural crops	1,524
Total area used for "field' crops	39,986
Total	41,510

Source: *The Comprehensive Development Plan for the City of Luxor*

On large farms both feudal and capitalist class structures constitute sugar-cane cultivation. Farmers who devote significant acreage to sugarcane hire workers, and this would constitute a capitalist class process. Landless work-ers harvest sugarcane for large farmers in return for sugarcane leaves (which they used as feed for their livestock). The non-wage form of remuneration means that a feudal class structure constitutes this particular way of orga-nizing sugarcane cultivation. In both these cases, the performers of surplus labor are excluded from the appropriative and distributive moments.

By examining the ways in which labor practices are organized, we see that farm household enterprises in Luxor and Qena are the sites of numer-ous complex class structures, some more participatory than others. Inde-pendent class processes may constitute the activities of women involved in animal husbandry and dairy production; feudal class processes may con-stitute women's tasks in the daily maintenance and re-production of the family (as conceptualized by Fraad, Resnick and Wolff); communal class processes may constitute the production of wheat, cotton and sugarcane. Some of these same crops (such as cotton and sugarcane) may be character-ized by capitalist or feudal class processes when they are grown on large farms to be sold in commodity form to the market. Men from small family farms, who work for wages on larger farms but then also work alongside women and children on their own farms, hold more than one class posi-tion. They hold a capitalist class position as the exploited worker on the large farm, a feudal class position the "lord" at home, as well as the patri-arch who controls the distributive moment in communal class processes. In this rendering, capitalist activities appear to be one among a diversity of ways to organize economic activity.

Thus, each farm household-enterprise emerges as a site characterized by a complex class structure with men and women holding multiple class positions. Furthermore, each class process is *overdetermined* by other class processes as well as numerous nonclass processes such as social, cultural and religious processes that converge in the socially constructed notions of the family, gender and patriarchy.

Mitchell's study of Qena for example, reveals the ways in which the communal class process of sugarcane cultivation serves as a condition of existence for the other class structures on the farm. On questioning farmers as to the motivation for growing sugarcane, he finds that the prevalence of sugarcane, even among small farms in the region, which may only grow one to two feddans of the crop, is due to its significance as a consumption-smoothing strategy. For small subsistence farms, sugarcane is the only "cash crop." The state-run factories that process the cane offer a cash advance loan early in the year during growing season when farm incomes are at their lowest. This loan is part of the payment for their crop in exchange for a commitment to supply a specified amount of sugarcane. As Mitchell notes, small farms in the region "could not survive the growing season without the loan" (p. 25). The farmers use the loan not just to finance their sugarcane crop, but also the seeds and fertilizer needed for household crops and diesel for the irrigation pump. In class terminology, sugarcane cultivation *is a condition of existence for the other fundamental class process on farm-enterprises*, such as the cultivation of wheat, beans and vegetables. In other words, a crisis in the reproduction of the class and nonclass processes that constitute sugarcane cultivation, could lead to a crisis in the reproduction of the other class processes that ensure the livelihood of the region's farm-household enterprises and perhaps even the larger community.

This dynamic between class structures may account for the persistence of sugarcane cultivation in the region, despite recommendations by the World Bank and USAID to cut back on the production of sugarcane in Upper Egypt. Sugarcane has been a major crop in Upper Egypt since historic times. Conditions in Luxor (and Upper Egypt in general) are particularly suited to growing sugarcane. Upper Egypt enjoys many hours of sunlight, intense light, a heavy clay soil and significant differences in day and night temperatures. In addition, between May and September the temperature in the region is too warm for most field crops except sugarcane. A common practice in the area is to plant it once and harvest it five to six times since the cane stays in the ground for three to five to years.[25] Traditional knowledge of the skills and techniques used in cane production has been handed down for generations. Sugarcane production's place in the social and cultural fabric of the region today is ensured by the crop's role as a consumption-smoothing strategy among the predominant small family farms in the area; and as a way of organizing economic activity that allows members of a community to help each other out by exchanging their labor power. In other words, the class and nonclass processes involved in sugarcane production ensure the reproduction of the class and nonclass processes that constitute the various farm household enterprises in the region.

The significance of sugarcane for the local community is however, minimized in the dominant narrative of export-led development in the region. To the contrary, the CDCL for example, advocates cutting back cane production in the region. Although Egyptian sugarcane yields are the highest in the world on the basis of the standard growing season (by comparison the US ranks eleventh),[26] a World Bank study suggests that the cultivation of sugarcane is "not to Egypt's comparative advantage."[27] Moreover, the crop involves the intensive use of both arable land and water—both scarce resources in Egypt.

The CDCL identifies investment in high-value agriculture and agro-processing industries as a "key element in the strategy to meet the contemporary needs of Luxor residents" (p. 16). Research on soil and climatic conditions shows that there is much potential for high-value agricultural crops and that Egypt has a comparative advantage in these crops (World Bank, 1992). Hence, within the heuristic of the strategy of export-led growth, high-value agriculture is considered important for developing the region in terms of its export potential for the European and Middle Eastern markets.

However, the introduction of high-value agriculture is problematic for three reasons. First, the distribution of land is uneven and most farmers in the area hold plots of land that are too small to support high-value crops; second, high-value crops are dependent on agro-processing plants that require heavy initial investment. As I have already stated, according to official government statistics, 90% of farms in the region consist of small privately owned plots of an average size of 1.84 feddans (almost 2 acres). Unofficially, plots are often smaller due to fragmentation, as land has been divided among family members through generations. The CDCL's proposed strategy to introduce high value agriculture therefore, faces a major difficulty: high value crops such as strawberries and string beans need a minimum of 10 feddans to be cost effective; table grapes, mangos and dates need between 50 and 100 feddans.[28]

Secondly, the perishable nature of high value crops means that agro-processing plants need to be located nearby for packaging, storage and transporting to markets. Warehouses and distributional facilities have to be maintained to prevent crops from spoiling. There are however, currently no such facilities in the Luxor area. An average facility is estimated to cost between US $ 323,000 and $1 million.

The Comprehensive Development Plan for the City of Luxor remains fixated on how to promote exports for capital accumulation and economic growth without exploring the context in which these changes are to take place. This strategy calls for replacing traditional crops with high-value crops without specifying how it proposes to bring about the redistribution of land needed for the large-scale farming associated with High Value Agriculture or the large-scale investment in infrastructure that will be necessary to process, transport and market these highly perishable fruits and vegetables. Last but not least, the CDCL's policies promoting the phasing out of sugarcane fail to take into consideration the crop's significance in the economic and social fabric of village life.

Conversely, class analysis accounts for the complex ways in which economic activity is organized. It reveals moreover, how various class and

nonclass processes overdetermine each other, such that a change in a particular process (such as a reduction in nonclass revenues of credit from state-
owned factories) can affect other class and nonclass processes, leading to a
crisis in the reproduction of the household itself. An example that clearly
illustrates this is the "feminization of agriculture." Rising ground rent,
input costs and cutbacks in subsidies has created a situation whereby small
farm household-enterprises have experienced falling revenues simultaneously with rising costs. Men have responded by seeking non-farm employment, usually forthcoming from the government and construction sectors
in Upper Egypt (Adams 2001; Assad, 1999), leaving women in charge of
the activities on the small family farms. Although further research is needed
to study the ways in which these changes affect the performance, appropriation and distribution of surplus labor, it seems likely that where men are
absent for long periods (as they are when working in the construction sector) or gone altogether (reflected in the rising incidence of women-headed
households), there are independent and communal class structures arising
within family farms.

In the following section I detail the role played by the State in promoting the crisis experienced by farm household-enterprises. I argue that in
pursuing primitive accumulation strategies, the State is concertedly pursuing a vision of development that promotes exclusionary over participatory
economic practices.

The State's role in surplus production

Among the many roles of the Egyptian State in Luxor's economy (collect-
ing taxes, distributing goods and services etc) there are two that emerge in
a different light seen through the lens of class. First, class analysis reveals
the State itself is pursuing capitalist class processes and second, among the
diverse mix of agricultural practices that exist in the locality, the state is
specifically securing the conditions of existence for the prevalence of capitalist class processes in Luxor.

First, contrary to mainstream representations of the Egyptian state
as being "socialist," the state itself is involved in capitalist activities in the
region. Class analysis reveals that state-run enterprises exhibit complex
capitalist class structures. The region's state-owned and managed sugar
factories buy sugarcane from local farmers at a fixed price, process it to
make sugar and then sell it as a subsidized commodity to consumers. They
are therefore also sites where surplus labor is produced, appropriated and
distributed. In state-owned enterprises, state-appointed board of directors
appropriates the surplus value produced by the workers who are therefore
excluded from the moments of appropriation and distribution.

Second, in contrast to the historicist narrative of the CDCL, the advent of capitalism in Luxor is not a "natural" or evolutionary inevitability. Rather, among the diverse mix of practices that exist in Luxor, the state, through its capitalocentric policies, is specifically promoting and fostering capitalist ones, through: (i) the creation of "tourist processing zones" that fall under special jurisdiction rights and are exempted from taxation and labor laws, (ii) through land reform in the hope that larger farms will lead to large-scale, mechanized capitalist agriculture and (iii) through the discursive marginalization of Upper Egypt and *Sai'idi* identity that is effectively dispossessing people from the land that they have on for centuries. In class analytics terms, the state through both development policies and narratives of Egyptian nationalism is creating the class and nonclass conditions of existence for capitalist economic activities. The following sections elaborate on these strategies employed by the state to promote capitalist activities in the region.

Fostering Capitalist Activities through (a) the consumption of Ancient Egypt and(b)through the creation of "capitalist enclaves"

Dominant narratives of development Luxor have emphasized the region's significance as a site of globalization and capitalist growth (The Comprehensive Development Plan for the City of Luxor, p., 9). The State has promoted nonclass processes of ideology such as Egyptian nationalism, modernization and its accompanying practices of economic development to foster the growth of capitalist activities in Luxor. Where capitalist activities have taken hold in Luxor's economic landscape, they have done so in small gated communities, or tourist processing zones. These pockets of capitalism—much like the export processing zones in developing countries—in effect maintain a separation not only between tourists and local people, but also maintain a separation between the economic activities within the tourist resorts and those outside in the locality.

Mitchell documents how tourism services in Luxor—accommodations, meals, the sound and light show, trips to the temples, visits to the necropolis—have become increasingly packaged and mass produced in such a way as to allow the industry to maximize their revenue through the mass marketing and "consumption of ancient Egypt" (ibid, p. 204, 2002).[29] Provided by international firms such as Sheraton, Hilton and Movenpick, these "tourist villages" have gradually become self-contained gated communities, offering everything from restaurants, bars, shopping arcades, and swimming pools to their own tomb excursions and Nile cruises. These enclaves of material comfort and luxury, he notes, offer a jarring contrast to the poverty of Luxor's surrounding communities:

> The difference in wealth was so pronounced that the tourists' enjoy-
> ment could only be secured by their physical separation from the host
> community . . . The local population, except for a small elite, was
> excluded by the prices charged and the guards posted at the gate. To
> enter particular areas, such as the swimming pool or gambling casino, a
> foreign passport might be required (Mitchell, p. 198, 2002).

So severe and managed is this separation between tourists and the local communities that even as far back as in 1982, a World Bank survey of tourist satisfaction revealed two opposing views. Some tourists complained of the ferocity with which local peddlers tried to sell them their wares; others complained that their trip to Luxor lacked any meaningful contact with "real Egyptians" (ibid, p. 204, 2002). As a result of these survey findings, the World Bank recommended that not only should the local government issue no further peddlers' licenses, but that it should also set up visitor management schemes and minimize the local community's "unregulated contact with the tourists" (Ibid, p. 197).[30] Consequently,

> Separate river ferry and bus facilities were developed to isolate the
> movement of tourists from local traffic. An enclosed visitor center with
> its own restaurants and shops was to be built to enclose tourists wait-
> ing for transportation. In a village adjacent to Gurna the plans called
> for an elevated walkway to be erected through the middle of the ham-
> let, so that tourists could cross from the parking lot to the Pharaonic
> temple without touching the village itself (Ibid, p. 197).

The ramifications of these policy recommendations by the World Bank have been far-reaching. For one, current development plans for Luxor have been organized around the need to promote a certain type of tourism: the type that caters to wealthy tourists and involves the marketing and consumption of not just ancient Egyptian archaeological sites, but also luxurious resorts with golf courses, luxury cruises and excursions along the Nile, business facilities, shopping arcades, fitness clubs.

These tourism enclaves not only physically separate the local community from tourists (the local population is prevented from entering the resorts by high prices and "guards posted at the gates" (ibid, p. 198)), but also in effect secure the conditions of existence for capitalist class processes to prevail in the tourism industry. The US- or European-based hotel chains located within these capitalist enclaves fall under special jurisdiction rights whereby they are exempted from taxation, enjoy "labor costs that are more than competitive in the world-wide scale" and benefit from "outstanding profits in the tourism field" (ibid, p. 197). Moreover, the state has ensured that as much as possible, the revenues from tourism stay within the enclosures of the "tourist village," minimizing the access that local community businesses have to potential tourist customers:

> The grand Egyptian hotels that used to provide little more than spacious accommodations and an elegant dinning room were replaced by hotel complexes that offered three or four different restaurants and cuisines, several bars, shopping arcades, a swimming pool and fitness club, cruises, excursions, business facilities and evening lectures and entertainment (Mitchell, 2002, p. 198).

In other words, the Egyptian state, in its bid to follow an export-led strategy of economic development has not only pursued policies to secure the conditions of existence needed for capitalist activities in Luxor, but it has also buttressed these enclaves by systematically excluding the local communities. They are not only physically excluded from the walled tourist resorts, but through the creation of tourist processing zones, they are excluded from access to the wealth generated by the industry as a whole.

Promoting capitalist class process through land reform that has led to a re-concentration of land and a crisis in the class processes of farm-household enterprises

Since 1987, the State has been enacting policies to gradually foster the emergence of large-scale mechanized capitalist agricultural class processes. In 1987 the agricultural sector was the first to undergo market reforms, with almost all input prices (seeds, fertilizers etc.) and all farm-gate prices liberalized by 1992. More significantly, in 1992 the State enacted Law No. 96, the "New Tenancy Law." This law has effectively promoted the conditions necessary to secure capitalist class processes by restoring private property rights in the agricultural sector.

Until 1992, the trend in Egyptian agriculture had been moving towards reduced concentration in land ownership (Ireton, 1998). This trend had started as early as the 1930s, but had been accelerated by Nasser's Agrarian Reform law No. 178 in 1952. Legislation in 1952, then in 1961 and then again in 1969, placed ceilings on individual ownership of land to prevent it becoming concentrated in the hands of fewer and fewer landowners. Law No. 178 of 1952 confiscated 1 million feddans (1 feddan = 1.038 acres) from large landowners and then redistributed it in plots of 3–5 feddans.[31] It also changed the tenancy laws.

The main effect of the 1952 Agrarian Reform law under President Nasser was "not so much the redistribution of land, but the regulation of agricultural wages and land rent" (Muller-Mahn, 1998 p. 257) through the creation of a specific type of tenant property right known as *hiyaza*. The *hiyaza* established the institution of permanent landholdings for tenant farmers. Before the revolution, being a tenant involved paying 70% of annual profits to the landlord. After 1952 this was changed so that landlord and tenant were to receive equal shares of the profit from cultivation. The rental rate that tenants were to pay landlords was set at 7 times the land tax that landlords had to pay to the government. The Agrarian Reform Law also made it illegal to evict tenants, who were then effectively allowed to pass on their tenancy to their children. Hence, as Muller-Mahn notes: "Despite the annual rents that still had to be paid to the original owners, most tenants felt as if the land was theirs" (p. 257).

In class terms, tenant farming in Egypt comprise of a particular type of *feudal class process*[32] whereby the tenant for all real purposes "owns" the land, but pays part of their surplus value as ground rent and part as profit-sharing with the landlord. Under the *hiyaza* system of property rights, farm households distributed a part of the overall surplus they had produced in a year to landlords as ground rent. This proportion was fixed at 7 times the land tax. The *hiyaza* system also mandated that the profits from marketable crops were to be shared equally between the tenant and the landlord. The landlord's "right" to the tenant's surplus was maintained through non-class processes of feudal ideologies of fealty.

However, in keeping with the World Bank's calls to reform the institutional structure of the economy to promote private property rights, the Egyptian People's Assembly passed the new tenancy law—Law No. 96 in 1992. Law No. 96 raised the rental rate from 7 to 22 times the land tax and made provisions for periodic re-negotiation. It also gave landlords the right to evict tenants after 1997 and sell their land. Thus the new tenancy law has effectively changed the nature of landownership patterns from the de-facto ownership instituted by the 1952 Agrarian Reform Law to private property rights that have led to land becoming even more concentrated.

What does this mean for changing class structure? For one, by giving landlords the right to evict tenants, Law No. 96 took away the *de-facto* ownership rights that had been in place since 1952. Law No. 96 also liberalized prices of seeds, fertilizer[33] etc, input prices that were previously subsidized by the government. It thus raised the overall cash needs of Egyptian tenant farmers. This has led to a crisis in the traditional class process of farm-household-enterprises.

This crisis can best be understood through a *class structural equation* (Cullenberg and Chakrabarti, 2001): an equation describing the revenues and expenditures of a site such as that of the farm household-enterprise in Luxor. The class structure equation accounts for the fact that every site of surplus production, appropriation and distribution is the site of flows of both revenue and expenditure. At any given point, the reproduction of the class and nonclass processes that constitute a site depends on the revenue side of this equation being greater than or equal to the expenditure side. If revenues are less than expenditures than there may be a crisis in the reproduction of one or more of the class and nonclass processes. The equation below accounts for the sources of revenue and the expenditures of a farm household enterprise such as the ones described in the preceding section:

$$SL + \Sigma\,SCR + \Sigma\,NCR = \Sigma\,SC + \Sigma X + \Sigma Y$$

The term SL represents the various forms of surplus labor produced and appropriated on the farm from numerous class processes. Thus surplus labor from the independent class process of animal husbandry, from the communal class process of raising wheat for household consumption, surplus value from the sale of sugarcane all constitute the overall surplus labor produced on the farm.

ΣSCR stands for the subsumed class revenue that flow into farms, such as dividends, ground rents, and merchant fees (usually obtained by wealthier farmers: for the vast majority of small farms and their families SCR will be low or zero). ΣNCR represents nonclass revenue such as government subsidies for fertilizer, water, electricity and loan support. NCR have been falling since 1987: in accord with the Government of Egypt's mandate to liberalize the agricultural sector, inputs such as fertilizer are no longer subsidized. There are also ongoing discussions as to how to charge farmer for irrigation water, indicating that nonclass revenue for farms are likely to continue falling. While sources of nonclass revenue for farm-enterprises are falling, through changes in property laws, the state is raising costs such as ground rent.

The term ΣSC is the sum of subsumed class payments such as taxes paid to the local government, merchant fees, ground rent and interest payments made to secure the conditions of the fundamental class process. The term ΣX represents the sum of payments made to secure SCR and ΣY, sum of payments made to secure NCR, such as state and local taxes etc.

For those farmers who rent their land, Law No. 96 has effectively raised subsumed class payment more than 3 times. On the other hand, NCR in the form of subsidized inputs have been falling. Hence, for a significant number of tenant farm-household-enterprises, their expenditures have exceeded the revenues from their various class processes: the surplus labor generated on farm-households is less than the sum of subsumed class payments, the sum of payments made to secure SCR and the sum of payments made to secure NCR.

$$SL + \Sigma\, SCR + \Sigma\, NCR < \Sigma\, SC + \Sigma X + \Sigma Y$$

The evidence of this crisis can be found in studies such as those of Muller-Mahn (1998), who found that throughout the nation about 800,000 farmers lost their landholding titles due to Law No. 96 in 1997.[34] If they are evicted from the land, they and their families will become landless workers.

How have Luxor's communities responded to this crisis? The rise in non-farm employment has clearly been one way to deal with the loss of access to land. As already noted, a large number of economic activities in the area are those that possess an independent class structure. Villagers in the area have also relied on tourists as a source of income, offering their services as local tour guides and charging tourists for access to the lesser tombs that are in the vicinity of their villages.

Fostering capitalist activities through the discursive dismantling of centuries-old customary property rights and effectively dispossessing people from their land.

Seen within the context of the larger narrative of Egyptian nationalism and its strategy to promote the "conditions of existence" for capitalist economic development, the State's attempts to remove and relocate the villages away from the vicinity of the temples, tombs and monuments, appear to be part and parcel of the larger strategy of exclusion. One of the three main objectives of the CDCL project summary document is to remove and relocate residents from archaeological sites to minimize the "human impact on the antiquities." There are two relocation projects that are currently underway in Luxor. One involves demolishing about one hundred homes currently located on top of the Avenue of the Sphinxes and relocating their residents to New Luxor; the second involves relocating the village of Gurna, which has grown up above the tombs of lesser nobles on the West Bank of Luxor. Physical plans for cities such as New Thebes had been drawn up such that the new settlements would be on the edge of the desert, away from the Nile, away from the villages and their cultivated fields and last but not least, away from the tourists. Once the local population has been moved out, and their houses destroyed, Luxor could then be turn into an "open air museum." "A few houses were to be left standing as examples of local architecture, and used to house artisans and craftsmen producing artifacts" (Mitchell, p. 198). This strategy is clearly in accordance with the World Bank's policy recommendations to minimize the local community's "unregulated contact with the tourists."

Indeed, Mitchell's account of development projects in the area reveals a history of forced attempts by the State to remove and relocate local residents from the vicinity of the antiquities. The first attempt to relocate the residents of Gurna took place in 1945 when an entire wall of a tomb disappeared. Members of the community were blamed for the theft and consequently, that year marked the first of many attempts to relocate the residents of Gurna to a "planned" village called New Gurna, between five and ten kilometers north of the tombs. Attempts to forcibly remove them were made again in 1992 and 1994. The villagers of Gurna have in turn resisted these attempts:

> On January 17, 1998, after several earlier skirmishes, a government bulldozer accompanied by tow truckloads of armed police moved into Gurna to carry out demolitions. A group of about three hundred villagers gathered, later swelling to several thousand, and drove the police back with stones, pushing their bulldozer into a canal. The police opened fire on the villagers with automatic rifles, killing four and leaving more than twenty injured"(Mitchell, 2000, p. 186).

Almost fifty years after the first attempt, in 2000, Gurna remained perched on the escarpment among the tombs. State plans to relocate them away from their cultivated land, their palm trees, their artisanal workshops and "their" tombs remain on-going to this day. For just as the State has been attempting to develop Luxor and its surrounding areas for decades, the local communities have been concurrently contesting and re-shaping the state's exclusionary policies through years of practical resistance.

Luxor as a site of resistance, contestation and rupture

In these "frenzied scenes in which local peddlers" try ferociously to "secure some small share of the tourist business," we begin to see glimpses of what Scott refers to as the "hidden transcript"—the behind-the-scene narratives of the communities of Luxor.

> . . . . The few occasions in which organized tourists encountered the local street, whether half an hour set aside for shopping in the Luxor bazaar or a five minute walk from the cruise ship to an archaeological

site through a strip of village, became frenzied scenes in which local
peddlers, merchants, and entrepreneurs tried to secure some small share
of the tourist business" (Mitchell, p. 198, 2002).

Though the State has awarded special jurisdiction status to Luxor
thereby securing the conditions of existence that allow for capitalism to
thrive (the property rights, labor laws, tax havens necessary to attract foreign direct investment), it has not been able to forcibly remove and exclude
the local communities from the initial site of wealth production: the tombs
and temples that attract the tourists in the first place. The local communities
have resisted this exclusion and contested for their customary rights to the
monuments, and the wealth generated by these monuments. These instances
of resistance constitute the concrete material struggles for the customary and
localized forms of property rights to the wealth generated by Luxor's tourism. That is, the local communities' hidden narrative of popular rights, values and outrage has manifested itself in everyday economic practices such
as their continued residence in and among the tombs and temples of Luxor.
Facing limited options of participating in the formal tourism industry, residents of Gurna have carved out their own spaces of participation.

Tourists in Luxor are increasingly interested in learning about local
communities and their way of life. As they make their way around the archaeological sites, young men offer to be their guides, promising them a visit to a
local home as part of the package. A visit to a home typically involves watch-
ing women make homemade bread in traditional clay ovens. The guides may
also take the tourists to the village souvenir shops in exchange for a com-
mission from storeowners who may well be part of their family. By resisting
forcible dislocation by the State, therefore, the residents of Gurna have tena-
ciously defended their claim to the area, its monuments and the beginnings
of what could become a model of community-based tourism.

Proximity to the monuments ensures access to tourists: living among
the antiquities allows the local community to act as "tomb keepers" and
tour guides—independent of the state and international travel agencies. In
other words, to contest their exclusion from participating in the tourism
industry, the villagers have asserted centuries of *de facto ownership-rights*
to some of the area's tombs and temples, through their continued *residence*
among the monuments. They have through this everyday act of resistance,
thereby forced the State and the global tourist industry, to *share* the social
wealth generated by tourism.

The villagers' resistance to the relocation projects has attracted considerable attention from the national media and, in the public discourse, the
State's and the media's representation of these people prevail: in the press,

in cinemas and in a number of popular television serials the communities in the area have been depicted as being against progress, modernization and the Egyptian national interest (Abu-Lughod, p. 168). Residents of Gurna who live on and among the tombs are depicted as being tomb-robbers who steal artifacts from the tombs, sell them and charge tourists for allowing them to view the tombs. They are portrayed as being "selfish and individualistic" for putting their own interests ahead of that of the Egyptian nation (ibid, p. 168). Their poverty and deprivation are interpreted as being part of their cultural outlook that prevents them from participating in the nation's economic development.

Ironically, there is little doubt as to whom the antiquities belong— the Egyptian nation, and the larger world (as a World Heritage site), but never the local communities.[35] Van der Spek (1998) by contrast presents a historical account of the relationship between the tombs in Luxor and the local communities, arguing that they have inhabited the tombs of Luxor for centuries. Mitchell (2002) notes "the debris of earlier excavations contains rich evidence of this long period of Coptic and early Islamic local life" (p. 203). Thus archaeological evidence suggests that the connections between "a dead past and a living community is part of the history of the Theban Necropolis" (ibid). While the narrative of mainstream development does not directly address the villagers' "hidden transcript" that claims their rights to the monuments and the wealth generated by tourism, it nevertheless has to contend with the fact that the villagers are contesting their exclusion by exercising those rights on a daily basis by refusing to relocate.[36]

Indirectly, the State continues to discredit the local communities' rights to the wealth generated by the region, laying claim to the idea that Luxor is "an international museum for everyone" (Minister of Tourism) and the necessity for "planned development" in Luxor given its global significance. These quotes reveal the underlying struggle for Luxor and its resources. They articulate the ideology underlying the historical and ongoing development strategies in the region. The ideology of Egyptian nationalism and its accompanying narrative of economic development articulate the justification with which the state, and through the state global multinational tourism corporations have laid claim to the wealth flows generated by Luxor's antiquities. These narratives constitute a concerted effort to discursively dismantle the local communities' centuries old customary property rights to the monuments.

CONCLUSION

This chapter is a case study of the dialectic between development planning policies, the narratives used to legitimize these policies and the hidden transcripts that have contested these policies in Luxor. Through dialectic Luxor and its surrounding areas are cast as the site of intensely fought struggles—both material and discursive. The dominant representation of the area is that of its role in the "economic progress" of the Egyptian nation-state. In this familiar narrative the region is represented as an engine of economic growth because of its ability to attract foreign capital through the global tourism industry.

Deconstructing this familiar narrative reveals that the viability of capitalist activity as an engine of growth is contingent on numerous overdetermined conditions of existence. The State has been creating these conditions through various processes such as institutional processes that foster separate "capitalist enclaves" that have special jurisdiction rights. The state is also attempting to promote capitalist activities in agriculture through new tenancy laws that have effectively led to a concentration of landholdings to promote larger mechanized farms. Lastly, through its control over the national media, the Egyptian State has been engaged in representational struggles: by appealing to the unifying forces of Egyptian nationalism over parochialism, it has been discursively dismantling the local communities' centuries-old customary rights to the monuments in the area. The local communities and their activities that have hindered the project of capitalist growth and development have been portrayed in these official narratives as being backward, uncivilized and in general an obstacle to the economic development and modernization of Upper Egypt.

Physically excluded from tourism enclaves, increasingly vulnerable to landlessness and periodically subject to attempts of eviction, the local communities have contested the State's plans for developing Luxor as an open-air museum. Their persistence in refusing to leave their fields, palm trees, houses and tombs constitute everyday acts of resistance against the exclusionary nature of the dominant narrative of economic development. By refusing to give up their rights to the area's tombs and temples, they are forcing the State and the tourism industry to share the revenue generated by Luxor's ancient cultural heritage. These sites of resistance therefore are the manifestations of the offstage discourse of localized, historically based forms of property rights and context-specific notions of economic justice.

Chapter Five
Revisiting Rotating Savings and Credit Association

> *How are survival and identity struggles marginalized and subordinated, even silenced by the hierarchy of economic efficiency? (Callari and Ruccio, 1996)*
>
> *Why is it that many ethnographic and anthropological studies depict women as important community figures who exert influence over the management of the household and wider social networks, yet the classic works on Egyptian politics and political economy barely allude to them? Where does all that power go? (Singerman, 1998)*
>
> *Unless we formulate new and different ideas of progress and development, the discursive space of policymaking will continue to be colonized by "neoclassical economic visions that celebrate the virtue of efficiency, competition and markets and the dynamic of capitalist growth (Chakrabarti and Cullenberg, 2003).*

Postmodern Marxian economists argue that non-capitalist activities are not the residual remnants of primitive, traditional practices, but that in fact non-capitalist economic activities always exist and mediate the various forms of capitalisms that have arisen in history. In doing so, they have, in effect contested the hegemonic representation of capitalism as the singularly viable form of economic activity. The imaginary equivalence between "capitalism" and "the economy," they argue, overlooks the fact that there are people who, in their everyday activities, are involved in a variety of "non-capitalist" practices. If capitalism is defined as a system with wage-labor, commodity output and profit accruing to the owners of capital, then

121

many of the activities that constitute the material basis for human existence, are non-capitalist, in that they involve physical labor that is not remunerated by wages and nor are the products of this labor sold as a commodity in exchange for money in markets. For instance, non-capitalist practices govern the way work is organized and output is produced in the (Fraad, Resnick and Wolff, 1994). Despite its significance in terms of the volume of output it produces to reproduce human beings on a daily and generational basis however, the household sector continues to be seen as being outside the sphere of the economy or at best, subordinate to it.

If Marxian economists have successfully contested the hegemonic representation of capitalism as the singularly viable form of economic activity, feminist economists have similarly contested the hegemonic representation of monetized activities as being constitutive of the Economy. They argue that women's unpaid work in the home and the community is a significant part of the economy, and that these non-market activities should be enumerated and included into our measurements of the economy.

For, for those interested in conceptualizing a participatory economy however, the strategy of "adding" the feminized spheres of non-market activities may not be adequate to the task of re-conceptualizing the economy (Cameron and Graham, 2003). Scholars informed by feminist epistemology, for example, also call for questioning the very epistemic categories that structure the capitalocentric discourse of economics. "It seems that the strategies of adding on and counting in might fall short of generating a feminist politics of transformation. They add to the picture of what contributes to the production of goods and services but they do not necessarily help us think differently about the economy" (ibid, page 13).

For instance, community-based informal finance networks such as rotating savings and credit associations (ROSCAs) transgress the gendered boundary between the monetized male sphere of production and the non-monetized sphere female of reproduction. Not only is the proliferation of ROSCAs in developing countries well documented, but so is the high incidence of women participating in these informal financial networks. The type of questions raised with respect to networks such ROSCAs, have tended to focus on their viability and the extent to which these funds contribute to capitalist economic development and capitalist activities more generally. Beyond what they contribute to the production of goods and services however, ROSCAs also constitute alternative, participatory ways of organizing economic activity.

Not only do they contest the masculinist discourse of neoclassical economics by transgressing the gendered boundary between the monetized male sphere of production and the non-monetized sphere female of reproduction, but they also provide us with indigenous, participatory models of how local communities collect, condense and then redistribute monetized wealth.

ROSCAS: UBIQUITOUS, PERSISTENT, NUMEROUS AND SIGNIFICANT

One common form of community-based, participatory economic activity that has been written about frequently in the development literature is the rotating savings and credit associations or ROSCAs. Although they may vary slightly in institutional form from context to context, these mutual financial aid societies are ubiquitous throughout the world. In Cameroon for example, ROSCAs are known as *tontines*; they are called *susu* in Ghana, *esusu* in Nigeria, *stockvel* in South Africa, *bishi* in India (Bouman, 1995). ROSCAs are also prevalent in Asia, Latin America and the Caribbean (Ardener and Burman, 1995).

Due to the difficulties involved in the measurement of the sums circulating in ROSCAs, the extent of their significance to an economy have been difficult to gauge. However, a number of studies have enumerated the number of people involved in ROSCAs in various developing countries. Schreider and Cuevas (1992) estimate that 80% of the population in Cameroon are members of rotating savings associations. Seibel (1986) suggests that 50% of the population in Congo and 50%-90% of the adult population in Liberia, Ivory Coast, Togo, Nigeria participate in ROSCAs.

While Africa is particularly noted for its "proliferation of mutual aid groups with a finance component" (Bouman, 1995, page 372), articles written in as early as 1960s describe the prevalence of ROSCAs in rural and urban Eastern Java, Japan, China and Vietnam. In his 1962 article, The Rotating Credit Association: A Middle Rung in Development Geertz suggests that the rotating savings association "is an intermediate institution" between "traditional" society and more modern forms of social organizations in the development process—"a product of a shift from a traditionalistic agrarian society to an increasingly fluid commercial one, whether this shift be very slow or very rapid" (page 260). Furthermore, writing half a century ago, he predicted that this form of an economic institution is "self-liquidating, being ultimately replaced by banks, cooperatives, and other economically more rational types of credit institutions" (page 263). Almost thirty years later, a series of works published in the 1990s, documents the fact that ROSCAs remain alive and well in developing countries. Buvinic and Berger's work (1990) as well as Otero and Rhyne's work (1994) describes the functions of ROSCAs in Latin American countries; Bouman's work (1994, 1995) discusses institutional variations in ROSCAs in West

African countries; Baydas, Bahloul and Adams' (1995), Singerman, (1995, 1997) as well as Hoodfar (1999) all illustrate the prevalence of ROSCAs in Egypt.

The work on ROSCAs in Egypt is especially of interest for its detailed ethnographic description of the communities that participate in ROSCAs, and because the work of Baydas, Bahloul and Adams' work enumerates the magnitude of funds as well as the number of people involved in these informal financial networks. Using data collected in Egypt in 1993, Baydas, Bahloul and Adams (1995) estimate that the equivalent to somewhere between half a million to a million US dollars circulate through the gam'iyas of people who work in the one particular institution that they surveyed. Of further interest is the fact that the employees of the particular institution they interviewed, worked at a bank! In other words, not only do people participate in ROSCAs in places where financial markets are "thin" or "missing," but they also exist among individuals who work in a formal financial institution[1] such as the Principal Bank for Development and Agricultural Credit (PBDAC) in Egypt.[2] Moreover, they estimate that half a million to a million US dollars circulate through the gam'iyas of the employees of the PBDAC, is a only small proportion of the amounts that circulate throughout Egypt's economy. Numerous studies attest to the fact that Egyptian households of all levels of income participate in gam'iyas, and that there is a strong savings ethic among low-income communities that are denied access to the formal financial sector (Singerman, 1995, 1999; Hoodfar, 1999). Their findings are especially interesting because they contradict the prevailing consensus in the development literature on Egypt. A number of studies have attributed the "gloomy" performance of investment in the Egyptian economy, to its "failure to mobilize enough savings" (Amin, 1995, page 22).[3]

Can we resolve this apparent contradiction between the failure to mobilize savings on the one hand and the huge sums of money that are circulating among community-based financial networks in Egypt? Or does this apparent "contradiction" give us epistemological insight as to how to go about re-conceptualizing the economy?

EVERYDAY SAVINGS PRACTICES: THE GAM'IYA IN EGYPT

ROSCAs, or gam'iyas as they are known in Egypt, are extremely popular and the literature attributes their popularity to a number of reasons. One reason for their popularity is that they provide poor people access to a financial network who would otherwise have little or no access to sources of credit. This is certainly true for the low-income households in the urban neighborhoods of Cairo. Most low to lower middle-income households cannot fulfill a bank's requirement for collateral, have no long-standing credit history and hence they have no access to the formal banking sector and formal sources of credit. For the vast majority of the people in these communities therefore, the informal savings and loan associations are crucial for purposes of consumption smoothing, for investment in small income generating projects, to finance the initial "key" money to have access to an apartment, to finance the costs of a marriage, to finance education, for sudden funding needs during crises (e.g. funeral expenses, theft, as a cushion against various shocks, prestation needs before id il-aDha, etc). Their accessibility is in part due to the small sums of money[4] required to participate in a gam'iya, and the fact that no collateral is necessary, only that the manager of the fund knows and trusts the participant.

A gam'iya may be formed among neighbors, workplace colleagues or community members. There may be any number of people who agree to be part of the association for some specified length of time (6 months, a year, 15 months etc). Before a particular gam'iya commences, members assign a leader and decide among themselves as to the sequence of who will receive the group funds every period. Then, every month (or two weeks) the leader collects the savings from the group and gives it to the member whose turn it is to use the funds. Thus a member can receive her "kitty" before completing her cycle of payments and she can negotiate with the group to receive her turn at a point when she expects to need it the most.

It is not uncommon, however, for Egyptians to participate in gam'iyas even if they do have access to formal sector intermediaries and have no immediate need to save or borrow money. In their study of 1,785 members in 51 gam'iyas, Baydas, Bahloul and Adams (1995) found that in addition to participating in these informal financial networks, almost half of them had also requested and received loans from the formal banking sector. These authors suggest that the popularity of the gam'iyas can be attributed to their flexibility, low transaction costs, low administrative costs and the fact that they avoid the costs involved in screening borrowers, monitoring the loans and enforcing their repayment.

Gam'iyas offer a great degree of flexibility in that members of a community can set up a fund to tailor their specific needs. Someone can set up a fund—or ask a "leader" to set one up in cases of an emergency (illness, funeral, migration expenses, wedding expenses etc) and arrange to be first one to receive the kitty. Individuals who cannot afford to participate in a specific gam'iya have the option to split a share with another person. They can also join a gam'iya involving smaller funds. Synchronizing gam'iyas with the participants' income flows also ensures maximum accessibility.

Gam'iyas involve little or no transaction costs since they are usually composed of people who either live in the same building or neighborhood or work in the same location.[5] Similarly, since the collected gam'iya funds are usually distributed to the member immediately, administrative costs are also insignificant. Last but not least, the fourth reason given in the literature to explain the prevalence and popularity of gam'iyas it that they solve at

> modest cost the fundamental problems in finance: agent incentives, mobilizing deposits, avoiding theft, screening and selecting borrowers, collecting loans, and applying sanctions. In large part, gam'iyas manage these complex problems because of prior knowledge that member have about each other and through their ability to exercise informal sanctions against those who fail to meet their obligations" (Baydas, Bahloul and Adams, 1995, page 658).

If gam'iyas are as popular as these studies indicate, and if participation in these financial networks are as "dense" as various authors estimate, why are these informal financial networks not given more importance in the development literature? Given that these community-based networks (throughout the developing world) represent indigenous, participatory mechanisms through which to collect and then redistribute condensed monetized wealth, why do they not configure more prominently in policy-making? More importantly, can the normative content embodied in these savings associations help us formulate new and different ideas of progress and development? Can they further the project of non-capitalist centered ways of re-conceptualizing the economy?

TRANSGRESSING BOUNDARIES

During the 1990s, the American University in Cairo published a series of ethnographic studies on low-income urban neighborhoods of Cairo (Singerman, 1995, 1999; Early, 1998; Hoodfar, 1999).[6] A common theme that emerges out of these ethnographies is the fact that the relative poverty and density of these urban neighborhoods have contributed to a distinct "alley culture" (Nadim, 1995). The population density of urban neighborhoods averaged 40,000 people per square kilometer in 1996, with the highest number of people per square kilometer (as much as 100,000 (Bayat, 1997) concentrated in the "popular" or Sha'abi quarters. Aside from the overcrowded apartments in four- or five-story narrow, terraced, brick-buildings, crisscrossed by unpaved alleys[7] these neighborhoods share a certain common sense of identity. The residents of these neighborhoods refer to themselves as the Sha'ab, meaning a collective people or folk, who characterize themselves as being the "reservoirs of national Egyptian identity" and "have a sense of their authenticity and believe that they embody the values and beliefs of the nation" (Singerman, 1997, page 14).[8] For the Sha'ab, preserving values and traditions involve preserving a Sha'abi way of life and maintaining the collective Sha'abi identity. At a fundamental level, on a day-to-day basis, preserving the Sha'abi identity involves the reproduction of the family and the Sha'abi community at large. The Sha'abi identity, affords these communities a focal point around which to organize collective efforts to improve the community's well-being.

The vast majority of the residents of Sha'abi neighborhoods are classified as being in the low to middle range of Cairo's income distribution. Economic reforms adopted since 1991 have imposed further hardships on these communities. Alongside liberalized markets and institutional reforms that have promoted bourgeois property rights, structural adjustment policies have cut food subsidies and social expenditures, they have forced early retirement for a large proportion of the employees of state-owned enterprises and generally contributed to rising unemployment as the much-desired private sector investment has not been forthcoming. These increased hardships have taken place in the context of continued systematic exclusion from political participation as well as from access to labor markets, housing markets and credit markets (Singerman, 1997; Hoodfar, 1999 and Ghannam, 2002).

As a consequence of this systematic exclusion and its accompanying impoverishment, economic activities in these neighborhoods are explicitly organized around the social goal of maintaining and reproducing the family, and more generally, the Sha'abi community at large. In other words, while mainstream economic discourse concerns itself with "visions that celebrate the virtue of efficiency, competition and markets and the dynamic of capitalist growth" (Chakrabarti and Cullenberg, 2003), the normative content embodied in the everyday economic practices of Cairo's popular neighborhoods, contests the idea that all aspects of life in modern Egypt will be prone to the capitalist logic of exclusion, efficiency and competition.

In this context one everyday economic practice that contests the logic of capitalism, is the Egyptian version of ROSCAs, the gam'iya, already discussed above. Variously described as informal, invisible, marginal, parallel or shadow activities, the gam'iyas are in fact ubiquitous, even among the low-income households of Cairo's popular quarters. Although

Egyptian households of all levels of income participate in these informal financial networks, studies by Singerman (1995, 1997 and Hoodfar, 1999) indicate that these associations play a crucial role as a survival strategy in low-income neighborhoods.

> Informal savings associations or gamai'yaat are extremely common in Sha'abi communities (and throughout Egyptian society). Huge sums of money circulate within them and provide credit on a scale that competes with the formal banking system (Singerman, 1997, 76).[9]

A prominent feature of ROSCAs in Egypt—and elsewhere—is that they are predominantly set up and managed by women (Singerman, 1997; Hoodfar, 1999). 83% of the gam'iyas surveyed by Baydas, Bahloul and Adams (1995) were organized and managed by women. In their concluding remarks the authors state that:

> We were amazed to find such dense participation in informal finance in Tersa and in PBDAC and to find people putting such large portions of their incomes in gam'iyas. We were also surprised to find women playing a dominant role in the forms of informal finance dealing with savings—the gam'iyas and moneykeeping—and informs that provide so called consumer credit. Clearly many women in the country are "finance literate." They have devised ways of processing efficiently small, short-term loans. These are services that the formal financial system is unwilling or unable to provide and they are services that both men and women wish to use (Baydas, Baloul and Adams, page 660).

The feminized nature of informal financial networks and the kinds of economic activities that they finance is no coincidence. The social construction of gender has much to do with the development priorities and notions of justice underlying the gam'iyas. Singerman (1997) finds that the gam'iyas "support an ethos of cooperation based on the principles of the familial ethos." By attempting to improve their material conditions through a community-based network, the funds raised through collective efforts remain within the community. As such the gam'iya represents alternative ways of organizing financial activity that privileges the well being of the community measured by its ability to maintain and reproduce itself.

Feminist theorists argue that economists have generally failed to see how traditionally female activities or dispositions have contributed to the economy. On the occasions that they are recognized, their contributions are often minimized or devalued. For instance, gam'iyas continue to hold the subordinate position of "informal" savings networks despite the fact that that significant sums of money circulate within them and provide credit on a scale that competes with the formal banking system (Singerman, 1997, page 76). As mentioned above, in their study of just 1,785 individuals in 51 gam'iyas Baydas, Bahloul and Adams conservatively estimate that upwards of US $500,000 circulate among the members of these particular networks per month. Could the subordinate position held by gam'iyas in the literature, have anything to do with their "feminized" goal of what Marxist economists term "reproducing the family"(Himmelweit and Mohun, 1977)?

Several ethnographies of urban communities in Cairo (Singerman, 1995 and 1997 and Hoodfar, 1999) indicate that the gam'iyas play a crucial role as a survival strategy for families in low-income neighborhoods. By keeping the savings generated by the members of a gam'iya within the community, we see that funds are frequently spent on what feminist economists have variously called "the other economy"(Donath, 2000). In her ethnographies of these communities, Singerman (1997) notes that her informants are conscious of the fact that creating their own financial network allows funds to remain within the community and put to use as families see fit.[10]

The rich contextual details of the ethnographic studies in urban Cairo provide insight into the logic underlying the prevalence and popularity of gam'iyas. While mainstream economic discourse and hence development policies undervalue re-productive activities such as child-care, care for the sick, the elderly and the daily activities that reproduce the family (see Folbre, 2001), the reproduction of the family is the dominant motive underlying the savings practices of the poor, low-income neighborhoods of Cairo. Reproducing the family and the larger neighborhood community is a question of survival. Yet, Singerman points out, this supposedly apolitical social goal rarely figures into the explanation of economic phenomena in Egypt— either from the perspective of how government policies affect the goal of reproducing the family or how the goal of reproducing the family affects government policy (Singerman, 1999).

The gam'iyas play a crucial role in this process by redistributing the community's savings for investment in these reproductive activities. These savings and loans practices allow households to engage in consumption smoothing strategies during economic exigencies, they finance expenses such as healthcare, education, as well as social events that require large financial outlays such as marriages and funeral etc, and, they serve as insurance against illness and unemployment.[11]

If recognition requires enumeration and if to be counted "in the economy" requires that economic practices involve monetary transactions, then
clearly Egyptian women play a significant role in accumulating savings,
re-investing them within their respective communities and managing these
community-based savings and loans associations. Because of this, through
their participation in ROSCAs, Egyptian women transgress the gendered
boundary between the masculinized, monetized sphere of production and
the feminized, non-monetized sphere of re-production.

Moreover, while mainstream development discourse concerns itself
with the efficiency of market outcomes that typically accompany capitalist growth, the normative content embodied in these community-based
savings networks suggest alternative, feminized visions of economic
progress. The significance of these community-based financial networks
is overlooked because they contest the capitalist model of growth and
development espoused by the Egyptian State, as well as the hegemony of
capitalist values such as competitive individualism over collective identity. Informed by neoclassical theory, mainstream development policies
in Egypt have been advocating markets as efficient resource allocative
mechanisms for (capitalist) economic growth. Implicit in the privilege
accorded to markets is a valuing of the ethos of competition, efficiency
and the justice of "market outcomes" in terms of the distribution of a
society's resources. In Egypt, the ethos underlying the financial activities
of the gam'iyas offer ideas of progress and development that are different
than the notions of efficiency and competition embedded in neoclassical
visions of economic justice. The practices involved in the gam'iyas, articulate notions of progress that prioritize the local community's survival
and material well-being through cooperative efforts. They finance re-
productive activities, privileging non-capitalist process of the household
sector over those to do with "economic growth through industrialization." In other words, participation in these collective, community-based
ROSCAs allows people to allocate surplus value towards human provisioning and the reproduction of the family.

Susan Donath (2000) argues that feminist economists "need to
insist that there are two equally important economic stories or metaphors" (page 116). There is the one about competition and then there is
the one about "caring labor," which refers to the "care-work" involved
in sustaining children, elderly and other adults throughout their lives.
While public services provide some of this through employing people
in hospitals, schools and social workers, much of the work involved in
the direct production and maintenance of human beings are still done
by women. This is especially true in times of economic restructuring in

developing counties when government expenditures are cut and also in industrialized economies when there are retrenchments in government budgets for social spending (Dymski and Floro, 2000).

CAN ROSCAS FURTHER THE PROJECT OF NON-CAPITALIST CENTERED WAYS OF RE-CONCEPTUALIZING THE ECONOMY?

One could see the gam'iyas as a "parallel banking sector" in Egypt, parallel that is to the formal financial sector, filling in "missing markets" by providing financial and insurance services to low-income households that are under-served by the financial services. One could see them as "the middle rung" in development: institutions that exist on the way to some goal or end (the top rung in development). Numerous studies have documented their insti-tutional arrangements and measured their significance and have added to the picture of what contributes to the production of goods and services in a country, but does measuring their significance help us think differently about the economy?

Measuring their significance in terms of what they contribute to capi-talist growth and accumulation—or Gross Domestic Product more gener-ally—would constitute a capitalocentric view of these community-based financial networks. Characterizing ROSCAs as "the middle rung" in the evo-lution of a financial system, or as informal institutional arrangements that exist in the shadow of the formal financial sector, defines them in terms of their relationship to formal financial institutions. Loans made by the formal financial system (which in the case of Egypt, still remains dominated by the State) are primarily channeled into "productive investment," where produc-tive is defined in terms of rates of return on funds loaned and typically involve investing in capitalist activities. Economic discourses that characterize capital-ist practices as the only ultimately viable way of organizing economic activity, not only ignore the diversity of practices that make up a given economic land-scape, but they also promote an exclusionary way of organizing economic activity that does not necessarily contribute to a community's well-being.

For instance, accounts of Egyptian women's participation in the economy remain focused on their participation or non-participation in the paid labor force. However, women's entrance into the paid labor force may not necessarily be "liberating" if they have to work under exploitative and dehumanizing conditions. Defining agency as being able to work outside the home overlooks the cost incurred by women in terms of their "second shift" (Hoschilde, 1989) at home, and the fact that the invitation to partici-pate in the capitalist "global assembly line" is an invitation to participate in a rigidly hierarchical and under often physically oppressive working conditions (Fernandez-Kelly; Ong, 1997). By contrast, gam'iyas provide loans to its members for a diversity of economic practices, some of which may be hierarchical and exploitative, but some may not. The women themselves organize some of the activities, and the work involved in them. In these instances, the woman in question determines the boundary between surplus and necessary labor, the conditions under which she will perform the surplus labor, and how she will distribute the surplus labor.

Rather than defining gam'iyas in terms of the extent to which they finance (or do not finance) capitalist activities (and hence capital accumulation and growth), can we define them by their own independent logic? Moreover, why continue to devalue gam'iyas and the values they embody by characterizing them as "informal" and hence of secondary importance to the formal financial sector? Why continue to minimize the significance of the daily and generational reproduction of the family, when clearly, the funding of these activities are prioritized by local communities through their participation in ROSCAs?

CLASS ANALYSIS OF URBAN CAIRO

Class analysis shows that capitalist class processes coexist among a heterogeneity of ways to organize the performance, appropriation and distribution of surplus labor in Cairo. This "de-centering"narrative reveals the fact that non-capitalist activities are not just residual, or embryonic capitalist practices, but coexist alongside capitalist activities and are a constitutive feature of a modern economy. Using the distinction between necessary and surplus labor, any given economic practice can be categorized according to the extent to which those who produce surplus labor participate in its appropriation and distribution. The language of class highlights surplus distribution as a potential object of political struggle.

Instances of Independent Class Processes

The 1998 Egypt Labor Market Survey shows that of the 4.9 million women in Cairo, only 779,000 women work in the paid labor force. The vast majority, 3.4 million are categorized as people who "don't desire work." Almost half of them cite their status as "full-time students" as their reasons for not desiring work. More than half of them cite their status as "housewife" as their reason for not desiring work. In the context of the popular, low-income neighborhoods of Cairo however, being a housewife does not preclude being self-employed, or working out of one's home, making and selling clothes and food to the immediate community.

Table 5.1. Labor Force Status of Women in Greater Cairo

Greater Cairo	1998 (in thousands)
Population of Women	4,937
Employed	779
Unemployed	188
Don't Desire Work	3,414

Reason for not desiring to work

Greater Cairo	1998 (in thousands)
Housewife	1,799
Full-time student	1,492
Other reasons	122

Source: The Egypt Labor Market Survey, 1998.

As Ibrahim (1983) points out, the popular Arabic meaning for housewife (*sitt al-bayt*), is inclusive of the notion of women working in a variety of home-based cash generating activities. In the context of the low-income urban neighborhoods in Cairo, raising rabbits, chickens, doves and petty retail trading is frequently cited as a significant source of household income:

> Umm Shadia was one of the many women whose home was the base for her income generating activities. She traded in clothing and bed sheets and she also raised chickens, rabbits, and pigeons for retail to neighbors. She earned an income of 80–100 pounds per month, while her husband's total salary was 60 pounds. However, she considered herself a "housewife" only and insisted that her daughter must receive formal education to be qualified to become workingwomen. Her case was typical of many women engaged in varieties of home-based cash-earning activities (Hoodfar, 1999, page 110)

Hoodfar goes on to note that her informants were not perceived as "workers" despite the fact that they were frequently putting more labor hours into family businesses and, in some cases earning more income than their "worker" husbands. Clearly, the meaning of *sitt al-bayt* (the Arabic for housewife), in this context does not conform to the public/private dichotomy between paid and unpaid work. A "working woman" is usually one who leaves her home for a paid job; in this context however, a housewife can be earning income without leaving her home. This is crucial for household survival given that going out in public requires that women meet certain patriarchal gender norms.

In class analytic terms, women involved in raising rabbits, chickens, doves and petty retail trading would be classified as being involved in an independent class process. Under this way of organizing economic activity, the worker performs, appropriates and distributes her own surplus labor. In other words, a woman who raised chicken for example, may sell the chicken to a neighbor. Typically in this scenario, she does not pay herself wages, but she does appropriate the surplus value from the sale of her chicken. Thus, the independent class process may involve non-wage remuneration for the work involved, it may be distributed in commodity form but it does not exclude the worker from appropriating her surplus labor. Alternatively, the woman may have slaughtered the chicken for her own family's consumption, in which case the output would have been distributed in non-commodity form. In either case, the independent class process does not exclude the worker who has raised the chicken from participating in the appropriation and distribution of surplus labor and is therefore a non-exploitative and non-capitalist way of organizing economic activity.

Instances of State-Capitalist and Private-Capitalist Class Processes

By contrast, the capitalist class process involves practices whereby each worker in a capitalist enterprise produces in a day enough wealth to sustain her- or himself (for which he or she is compensated in the form of wage) and also a surplus, which is appropriated by the individual capitalist or by the board of directors of the capitalist firm. Since the physical product of surplus labor (or the monetary value of it) is appropriated by someone other than the direct producer of this surplus labor the worker is said to be in an exploitative relation with the appropriator of surplus value. Of the 779, 000 women who were "employed," 328,000 said they worked for the "private" sector. These women were most likely involved in a capitalist class process, where they were remunerated in wages, their output was distributed in commodity form and the owners of capital appropriated the surplus value generated in the process. 367,000 women worked for the "government"—meaning they were paid in wages, their output was sold in commodity or non-commodity form depending on the type of service they provided (school teaches for example, are paid in wages, but since primary education is free, their output is distributed in non-commodity form). If the surplus labor produced at these sites is appropriated by the State or a board of directors (as in the state-owned enterprises) then some of these women, as well as the 74,000 who said they worked for the public sector, are involved in state capitalist class processes. These too are exploitative in the sense that those who produce surplus labor are excluded from the appropriative and distributive moments.

Table 5.2. Distribution of Women Workers by Sector

Greater Cairo	1998 (in thousands)
Government	367
Public	74
Private	328
Other	8
Total	777

Instances of Feudal Class Processes

As conceptualized by Fraad, Resnick and Wolff (1994), the tasks involved in the daily maintenance and re-production of the typical patriarchal family constitute a feudal class processes. Under this way of organizing economic activity, the social construction of gender, prevailing notions of the patriarchal family give rise to a class process where women perform surplus labor (cooking, cleaning, child rearing etc) and the output is distributed in non-commodity form. In his role as the patriarch or "lord" of the house, the husband appropriates the surplus labor of his wife. However, Hoodfar and Singerman's ethnographies indicate that further research is needed to better understand the intersections of gender, patriarchy and power over the appropriative distributive moment of surplus labor. Because of the religious and cultural preeminence accorded to the re-production of the family, women in Cairo have asserted their entitlement to the household's surplus labor by appealing to Islamic laws concerning the family.

Furthermore, the class structure of numerous households may be changing with the rising incidence of female-headed households in Cairo. The absence of male authority may result in the failure to reproduce non-class processes such as notions of patriarchal power and the traditional social construction of gender. Since these nonclass processes made up the conditions of existence for feudal class processes, household class structures may transition into independent or communal class processes, if women and children collectively perform, appropriate and distribute surplus labor. The consequent new relations of power and patterns of property ownership are likely to affect the way surplus labor is produced, appropriated and distributed in these female-headed households, and perhaps bring into existence alternative, yet-to-be-conceptualized class processes. The ways in which in power relations, gender norms and property ownership articulate with various class processes in female-headed households promises to be an interesting direction for future research.

By examining the ways in which labor practices are organized, we see that households in the popular Sha'abi quarters of Cairo are the sites of numerous complex class structures, some more participatory than others. Independent class processes may constitute the activities of women engaged in raising chicken, goats and rabbits as well as in petty trade. Feudal and communal class processes may constitute women's tasks in the daily maintenance and re-production of the family. Family members most likely hold numerous class positions: for example, a man may hold a capitalist class position as the exploited worker in private or state capitalist firm as well as a feudal class position as the "lord" at home. Similarly, a woman may hold a feudal class position as the "feudal serf" position as a wife in a typical patriarchal family as well as an independent class position in her business as a neighborhood seamstress. In those instances where Cairene women are asserting their Islamic rights to their family's wealth and income, their may be communal class processes arising. Thus, each class process is overdetermined by other class processes as well as numerous nonclass processes such as social, cultural and religious processes that converge in the socially constructed notions of the family, gender and patriarchy.

In this class-based rendering of Cairo's Sha'abi neighborhoods, capitalist activities appear as merely one among a diversity of ways to organize economic activity. Moreover, capitalist activities do not emerge as the only viable economic form: indeed, the "familial ethos" that pervades the Sha'abi neighborhoods with its emphasis on the maintenance and reproduction of the family, fosters a collective over an individualist approach to economic practices. Nowhere is this collective approach to formulating economic survival strategies more obvious than in the Sha'abi communities' use of gam'iyas.

GAM'IYAS AS SUBSUMED CLASS PROCESSES: SOURCES AND USES OF FUNDS

In the low-income neighborhoods of Cairo, the struggle for the material basis of daily existence becomes the social goal of reproducing the family. In order to reproduce the family, people have to save huge sums of money to a) finance a wedding party b) find a place for the newly married couple to live c) buy furniture and other household effects. As Singerman puts it, "Because Egyptians labor so hard to accumulate "marriage capital" they have developed an impressive savings ethic. Almost every wedding in these areas was financed in part by a gam'iya" (page 124).

If financial institutions are conceptualized as sites where a community's wealth is "condensed and collected" (Biewener, 2001) then gam'iyas represent participatory ways of distributing this condensed form of a community's wealth. Gam'iyas provide us with localized models of how communities channel and invest their collective surplus labor in their community. Gam'iyas therefore, constitute what Resnick and Wolff refer to as a subsumed class process.

Surplus labor produced under various conditions by individual members of a community is then collected and distributed in a participatory manner. For example, surplus labor from raising poultry under an independent class process, from working for a family food stall under communal class process, or even from a capitalist class process is channeled into a gam'iya by men and women who are participating members. Once condensed into a gam'iya's "kitty," each receiving member then uses this collective surplus as they see fit. Gam'iyas constitute the conditions of existence for the numerous class processes involved in reproducing the social institution of the economy. In this de-centered discourse, the practices involved in the reproduction of the household are of importance, not because they support and sustain capitalist activities, but rather, in this class based rendering of what constitutes the economy, capitalist activities exist as merely one among the many economic practices that maintain and reproduce the family.

In Sha'abi neighborhoods, huge sums are spent on creating the conditions of existence for those class processes that maintain and reproduce the family. One very visible example of an economic activity financed by gam'iyas in Cairo's popular neighborhoods is the construction of "informal housing." Between 50–80% of the housing constructed since 1960 have been built illegally, without building permits sanctioned by the state. Although over the years, the State has bulldozed a few of these illegal settlements, it "has not been able or willing to control this massive growth in informal housing" (Singerman, 1997, page 131). Illegally constructed settlements are rarely prosecuted due to the prohibitive cost involved in enforcing the law. Nor do these communities have access to running water, sewerage, electricity, transportation grids, or health and education services. Over time however, the continued existence of these informal settlements, have meant that communities have either negotiated with the State to procure access to services in return for taxes, or they themselves have paid for the procurement of these services.

In the highly cramped quarters of these densely populated neighborhoods, procuring living space becomes a crucial part of the process of financing a marriage to start a new family. Consequently, Cairo's urban landscape has witnessed the proliferation of illegally added-on rooms on the roofs of existing buildings, or on adjoining land usually owned by the state or some absent party. "The growth of illegal settlements and communities, due in part to the seemingly innocuous social goal of reproducing the family presents a political and economic predicament, if not challenge, the Egyptian state" (Singerman, page 131).

CONCLUSION

From a mainstream economics perspective, rotating savings associations are nascent forms of community banks, credit unions that provide financial services to underserved, low-income households. Not only do ROSCAs exist worldwide, but throughout the world, these funds have some remarkably common uses. Funds borrowed from ROSCAs are often used to finance the purchase of durable goods, move into a new house ("key money" and deposit), invest in a business, finance funerals and weddings, and support migration as an economic strategy (Bouman, 1995). Within the paradigm of capitalocentric mainstream economics, ROSCAs may be seen as an interesting case of market failure, stepping in fill in the gaps left by missing markets or ineffective states. Dupuy (1991) for example, argues that they have taken over responsibilities of social security, public investment and resource distribution from bankrupt states in West Africa

Policy implications that come out of studies such as these might call for gauging the prevalence of these financial networks and measuring the output financed by ROSCAs and evaluating their impact. The fact that women emerge as playing key roles in these community-based financial networks, acting as "bankers" by mobilizing savings, making small loans, screening potential gamai'ya members, and acting as a source of information on individual's credit worthiness, makes them more attractive for policymakers who are interested in pursuing gender sensitive development programs.

Measuring the significance and impact of ROSCAs in a given economy is a worthwhile goal for numerous reasons. These community-based financial activities (i) provide policymakers with a guide to viable ways of organizing participatory financial institutions in an economy where formal financial intermediaries are notoriously non-democratic; (ii) they stand to dispel the myths regarding the savings habits of low income households; (iii) they bring to the forefront the fact that women are very able "bankers"; (iv) they allow local communities to mobilize savings and loans at low transactions costs and (v) allow mobilized funds to remain within the community—or at minimum enable community members to allocate their saving as they see fit.

While "adding on and counting in" the significance of rotating savings and credit associations is clearly a worthwhile goal for the above mentioned reasons, the type of questions raised with respect to networks such ROSCAs, have tended to focus on their viability and the extent to which these funds contribute to capitalist-centered economic development and capitalist activities more generally, which, Marxists have argued, are non-democratic and exclusionary in their allocation of the fruits of development. By remaining within a capitalism-centered epistemology, mainstream analysis of ROSCAs characterize these institutions as being fixed in a "subordinate, under/devalued position vis-à-vis the 'core' (capitalist) economy" (Cameron and Gibson-Graham, 2003, page 13–14) and its supporting financial sector.

ROSCAs transgress the boundaries between the non-monetized household sector and the monetized 'core' economy by channeling a community's social surplus into everyday economic activities that sustain and reproduce the family on a daily and generational basis. In doing so, not only do they break part the dichotomy of the masculinized/market realm and the feminized/household realm that pervades mainstream economic discourse, but they also provide examples of efficiently provided participatory, community-based financial services that prioritize allocating surplus to the non-capitalist goal of reproducing the family and the larger community. In doing so, ROSCAs prompt us to reconsider what constitutes the economy, productive investment, economic growth, progress and development.

Conclusion

During the last two years democratic movements have made demands for greater political and economic participation in Egypt—in spite of repeated crackdowns by the State. A new visible and vocal popular movement *Kifaya,* has emerged on the scene; a number of judges in Cairo have recently spoken out against the State's efforts to control the judiciary system; and in July 2006, 25 leading newspapers went on a concerted strike to protest the State's on-going attempts to criminalize investigative journalism. Even more noteworthy is the fact that during the 2005 elections, the Muslim Brotherhood successfully won 20% of the seats in the parliament. In this period of vigorous democratic activity and a climate of heightened public awareness, what concepts of participation are circulating in the discursive space of economic development? Is there a space where we can engage democratic movements as they struggle to voice local notions of progress and development?

Prevailing models of participatory development in Egypt offer local communities limited options of participation that at best ratify the exclusionary policies of capitalist economic growth. While the Egyptian State's previous social contract approached subjects of development as passive recipients of the state's welfare policies, current approaches emphasize participation through markets in the pursuit of self-interest. In advocating participation as "access-to-markets," the approach continues to tacitly support the view that local communities have no alternative but to ratify a meager concept of participation. Markets as vehicles of participation offer limited exit-based notions of participation and do not address the open-ended possibilities of "participation as process." Exercising the prerogative to boycott Luxor's labor market for instance, is not equivalent to participating in the decision-making process affecting the way that the tourism industry is organized in the region. To what extent is an individual empowered by refusing to be exploited by a capitalist class process when she has no other option? Are there non-exploitative alternatives for local communities to participate in the area's tourism industry? And what spaces of participation have they carved out for themselves?

Framing the participation debate between the public avenues of voting or the private pursuit of self-interest through markets however, leaves little discursive space for alternative community-based and identity-driven notions of participation. An outgrowth of densely populated and highly integrated urban communities in Cairo, informal networks represent alternative forms of associational life. These reconfigurations of civil society provide context-specific models of communities organizing economic activity to work towards collective ends. On-the-ground participatory ways of organizing surplus production, appropriation and distribution provide indigenous models of participatory development practices.

Rising unemployment in urban areas, resurgent popular movements, persistent levels of human deprivation in Upper Egypt, increased disparities between wealthy foreign tourists and their impoverished host communities indicate that these alternative possibilities should be explored with some urgency. These coordinated efforts to attain collectively agreed upon goals also beg the question that if these communities were not preoccupied with resisting marginalization, exclusion, and dispossession, what might locally defined notions of progress and development look like?

Notes

NOTES TO THE INTRODUCTION

1. As Michael Watts ironically comments: "capitalism will bring everyone up to the current levels of material welfare of North Atlantic states" and liberal democracy will spread "like wildfire everywhere" (Watts, 1995, p. 45). To the contrary however, Watts argues that "the collapse of communisms in Eastern Europe and the former Soviet Union coupled with growing market integration has not produced the unambiguous ascent of a single model of capitalist democracy or the end of history but rather the aggressive assertion of difference in the guise of ferocious nationalisms and ethnic violence" (ibid, p. 45).

2. Majid Rahnema describes how the narrative of economic development had widespread appeal in the aftermath of World War II. Development as (capitalist) economic growth appealed to the elite ruling classes, the masses of the newly independent nations, as well as the former colonial powers who were hoping "to maintain their presence in the ex-colonies, in order to continue to exploit their natural resources, as well as to use them as markets for their expanding economies" (1997, p. ix,).

3. *Madness and Civilization: A History of Insanity in the Age of Reason* (1965) and *The History of Sexuality* (Foucault, 1978).

4. For instance C.L. R James in *The Black Jacobins* (1989) documents how both the 18th century French government and the French press systematically silenced the Haitian Revolution of 1791–1803. Led by a barely literate slave named Toussaint L'Ouverture, the Haitian revolution became the model for consequent Third World liberation movements.

5. I am referring here to earlier critiques of development by Paul Baran (1973), Andre Gunder Frank (1969) and Immanuel Wallerstein (1974).

6. I discuss and illustrate which activities constitute "capitalism" in Chapter Four. For now, however, I will follow the postmodern Marxist definition of capitalism as a system with wage-labor, commodity output and profit accruing to the owners of capital.

7. The term is related to the feminist notion of *phallocentrism,* which refers to the phenomena whereby all references to femininity is derived from its relationship to masculinity. "Whenever women or femininity are conceived in terms of either an identity or sameness with men; or of their opposition or inversion of the masculine; or of a complementarity with men, their representation is phallocentric" (Grosz, 1990, p. 150).

8. The Marxist term social totality is distinct from the notion of society in that the term social totality underscores the Marxist view that economic, ideological and social elements are all dynamically interrelated. According to Bottomore, a social totality exists "in and through those manifold mediations and transitions through which its specific parts or complexes are linked to each other in a constantly shifting and changing, dynamic set of interrelations and reciprocal determinations" (1983, p. 537).

9. Cullenberg and Chakrabarti (2003) define this constant flux and change in class structure as *transition* (p. 167). They discuss the Marxian concept of transition in *Transition and Development in India,* New York: Routledge.

10. Postmodern Marxists distinguish themselves from classical Marxism through this *non-historicist* understanding of the development of a social totality. *Historicism* is the "rational ordered progression of society moving from a pre-ordained origin towards a teleological ending" (Chakrabarti and Cullenberg, p. 296, 2003). For example, the idea that human history can be seen as a narrative that describes the evolution of the modern citizen-subject out of barbaric prehistory follows a historicist logic. That colonized societies "were assigned to the prehistory of the West" (Lowe and Lloyd, 1997, p. 4) is also historicist.

11. McCloskey (1994) notes that the meaning of the word "Science" in modern English is distinct from what it means in other languages such as German, Finnish, Swedish, French, Italian, Spanish, Dutch and Hebrew. Whereas in these latter languages science means "systematic inquiry" (p. 56), in modern English it has come to be restricted to only the physical sciences such as physics, chemistry and biology, thereby excluding knowledge "earned beyond the laboratory" (p. 57). Thus, remarks McCloskey, "Science must enumerate . . . Science must be mathematical. . . . Science must test hypothesis. . . . Science must experiment" (ibid, p. 59). She traces the history of how demarcating scientific inquiry from non-scientific inquiry became one of the projects of modernity. In Chapter Two, I will argue that by claiming to be "scientific," the discourse of economic development has effectively silenced alternative local ways of knowing as being "non-scientific" (or, as Marglin (1990) points out, [economic policies based on] "our science" is better than "their superstition").

12. Richie Howitt (2002) for example documents how the persistence of indigenous rights among Native American Nations in the United States and Canada as well as the Maori in New Zealand, have influenced public policy, constitutional reform and resource management. Moreover, he notes that indigenous nations have become increasingly vocal about their opposition to adopting Western institutions that are detrimental to traditional ways of "knowing" and "being."

13. I am not suggesting that the identity-difference politics of feminist struggles, indigenous movements, anti-racist, anti-imperialist or anti-globaliza-
tion movements are all integrated through some over-arching principle.
Indeed, one of the problems faced by theorists of new social movements
is that "identity politics" is divisive: identities of gender/race/class are very
often constituted through essentializing discourses that exist in conflict
with one another. Critics of postmodern theory suggest that because of the
cacophony of voices that are heard in the narratives of new social movements, the implications of social constructivism are in danger of becoming
an incoherent, "mindless empiricist celebration of pluralities" (Benhabib,
2004, p. 6). In *From Identity Politics to Social Feminism: A Plea for the
Nineties* (2004), Benhabib puts forth an eloquent argument for "identity-
transcending group solidarities."

14. Unlike the European welfare states, the US had to contend with a multi-
ethnic and racially divided polity. Seyla Benhabib writes, "Throughout the
early seventies, the American polity was faced with the dual challenge of
redistributing public goods like health, education, welfare housing and
transportation on the one hand, and of carrying out a Civil Rights agenda
for the elimination of discrimination based on race, gender, ethnic, religious and linguistic identities on the other. The most contested issues of
the seventies like busing, school desegregation, public housing and an end
to discriminatory employment practices combined issues of redistribution
with the realization of the Civil Rights agenda" (2004, p. 7).

15. James C. Scott's uses this phrase in his study of the enclosure movement
and poaching on the "King's land" in 18th century England (*Domination and the Arts of Resistance*, 1990). As the state began to appropriate
common land and restrict villagers' rights to hunt, fish, or using the land
as pasture, local communities responded by "the increasingly massive
and aggressive assertion of these rights, often at night and in disguise."
Poaching by villagers was so common and on such a large scale, that
Scott argues that this form of practical resistance to state policy must
have been justified by "a lively backstage transcript of values, understandings and popular outrage to sustain it" (1997, p. 316). He refers
to this suppressed narrative as the "hidden transcript." In other words,
though "there were no public protests and open declarations of ancient
forest rights in a political environment in which all cards were stacked
against the villagers," they were in effect contesting state policy though
practical forms of resistance such as poaching the game that they felt was
rightfully theirs to take. Chapters 4 and 5 examine the hidden transcripts
of everyday economic practices as instances of resistance to exclusionary
state capitalist policies.

16. As Bowles and Gintis (1987) point out that narratives that contest the neoliberal worldview are more likely to employ the language of rights associated with the French *Declaration of the Rights of Man* and the American
Bill of Rights than that of the *Communist Manifesto*.

17. Sabah Mahmoud (2000) documents the revival of Islamic movements
across Cairene society, especially among women and the youth. Mosques

have traditionally provides a public gathering place for men and women to meet (separately) to discuss Islamic notions of progress and social justice.

NOTES TO CHAPTER ONE

1. Neoliberalism has been heavily criticized both for its theoretical underpinnings as well as the effectiveness of its policies (see for instance Chang and Grabel (2004); Stiglitz (2002)). Nevertheless, the neoliberal worldview remains entrenched in the World Bank and especially IMF policy circles. James Galbraith notes that as more and more countries under neoliberal policy regimes experience crises, they are typically seen as "exceptions to the rule" (Galbraith, 1999, page 1). Thus for example, Mexico was an exception to the rule because of the revolt in Chiapas; South Korea, Thailand and Indonesia were exceptions because they suffered from "crony capitalism"; and then Russia was an exception because, as Galbraith wryly remarks, of "Dostoyevskian criminality" (Galbraith, 1999, page 1). Galbraith points out that "when the exceptions outnumber the examples, there must be trouble with the rules." "Where," he asks, "are the continuing success stories of liberalization, privatization, deregulation, sound money and balanced budgets? Where are the emerging markets that have emerged, the developed countries that have developed, the transition economies that have truly completed a successful happy transition? Look closely. Look hard. They do not exist" (ibid).

2. While even the most stalwart supporters of neoliberalism now shy away from advocating completely unfettered flows of financial capital, they nevertheless still guard the core tenets of the Washington Consensus: the policies, institutions and practices that promote and foster [capitalist] economic growth. Kuczynski and Williamson for example, in *After the Washington Consensus* (2003) add conditions such as good governance, anti-poverty measures and capital controls, but maintain "the way forward is to complete, correct and complement the [neoliberal] reforms of a decade ago, not to reverse them" (page 18). Rodrik (2002) refers to these additions as "the Augmented Washington Consensus"

3. The corporatist model of countries such as Sweden and Norway for example, are often cited as having taken a qualitatively better path to industrialization than countries such as United States and United Kingdom (Marshall, 1995). Cullenberg (1992) attributes the quality of life in the northern European countries as characteristic of what he terms 'benevolent capitalism' vis-à-vis the repressive regimes of states such as the former Soviet Union as 'hideous communism' (page 12). These are some of the examples of the heterogeneity of ways in which countries can 'develop.'

4. Using cross-national data, Rodrik draws attention to the fact that "participatory regimes are associated with significantly lower level of aggregate economic instability" (2001). Elsewhere he argues that the largest gains from global economic integration lie in the participation of workers in global labor markets—that is, "relaxing restrictions on the international movement of workers" (Rodrik, 2002, page 19).

5. I should note here that both Stiglitz and Kanbur were pressured to resign for (Kanbur was director until May 2000) their opposition to orthodox views within the World Bank. Stiglitz chronicles his conflict with the World Bank and the IMF in "The Insider: What I learned at the World Economic Crisis," *New Republic6*, April 2000 and in his book *Globalization and its Discontents* (2002).

6. *Voices of the Poor: Can Anyone Hear Us?* (Narayan, Chambers, Shah and Petesch (2000) draws on the pioneering approach to studying poverty based on the synthesis of applied anthropology, agro-systems analysis and rapid rural techniques of appraisal.

7. For an overview of the microfinance literature see Morduch (1999)

8. The principal-agent problem in economics refers to the uncertainty that arises when agents engage in contracts. Once a contract is signed by say a lender and a borrow, the central dilemma faced by the lender is whether or not the borrower will act in ways that will ensure the timely repayment of the loan. Because the borrowers actions may be unobservable, they may misuse or misallocate funds unless appropriate mechanisms are set. There is an extensive literature theorizing the actions of principals and agents under these conditions. See for instance, Kenneth Arrow (1985), Steven Ross (1973) and Joseph Stiglitz (1987).

9. See for instance Knack and Keefer (1997) "Does Social Capital Have an Economic Payoff? A Cross Country Investigation," *The Quarterly Journal of Economics.*

10. Fostering the start-up, growth and sustainability of micro-enterprises accords nicely with neoliberal ideology in general since micro-entrepreneurs are seen as people who "without any help from the state, make their own way and depend on themselves or their communities to survive" (Elyachar, 2002).

11. In Chapters 4 and 5 I shall argue that in the Egyptian context, certain community-based networks and ways of organizing economic activity are more participatory than market-based economic practices that tend to actually exclude large sections of Cairo's society.

12. Albert Hirschman, *Exit, Voice and Loyalty: Responses to decline in firms, organizations and states,* (1970).

13. An example of this phenomenon is the rising disparity that characterizes the US public school system where those who can afford to, move to neighborhoods where a healthy tax base supports better public schools. Children in low-income neighborhoods, with a lesser tax base are then "left behind" in under-funded schools, which are more susceptible to cutbacks in curriculum, high teacher turnover rates and a general deterioration in the education experience (Kozol, 2005).

14. Interestingly, the authors note that the Civil Rights Movement in the United States used the capitalist discourse of "anonymity of exchange and the irrelevance of identities" among parties involved in the buying and selling of commodities, to contest the "right of exclusion generally conferred by the ownership of property (Bowles and Gintis 1987, page 27). In other words, dominant notions of participation in the Civil Rights Movements remained very much within the confines of a capital-centered paradigm.

15. See for instance, Bowles and Gintis' "The Inheritance of Inequality," in the *Journal of Economic Perspectives, Vol. 16, No. 3, Summer 2002.*
16. See for instance Freedman and Medhoff (1984) and Kochan and Osterman (1994).
17. Stephen Resnick and Richard Wolff's (1987) is one of the first volumes to extensively develop the class analytical framework.
18. It also reveals a multitude of other, non-class processes that have to do with ideology and identity. These non-class processes are significant in their role in maintaining or subverting existing class processes and I will discuss them further in the following section.
19. Bowles and Gintis note that "Movements of the right—political turn of religious fundamentalism, nationalism the right to life movement and others—exhibit an equal focus on the cultural focus of politics (Bowles and Gintis, 1987, page 10).
20. See Callari and Ruccio (1996) for a discussion on Althusser's synthesis of Freudian and Lacanian psychoanalytic discourses on the "unconscious" with Marxian theory.

NOTES TO CHAPTER TWO

1. Bottomore (1983) cites August Comte (1798–1857) as the founder of positive philosophy, the project of which was to extend the methodology of natural science to the study of society. A combination of empiricism and rationalism, the influence of this intellectual movement on economics is felt most clearly in the importance given to demarcating scientific from non-scientific knowledge (see Caldwell, 1991; McCloskey, 1994). The production of knowledge that is "scientific" (in the Anglo-American sense of the word) involves observing social phenomena, quantifying them, formulating hypotheses, testing them, and then coming up with general laws to describe social behavior. This chapter explores the implications of positivist science for economic development.
2. For a discussion on postmodern currents and their influence on economics see Donald McCloskey, 1983, 1986; Jack Amariglio, 1988, 1990; Sheila Dow, 1991; Warren Samuels, 1991; David Ruccio, 1991.
3. For an incisive review of this literature see for instance the edited volumes by Cullenberg, Amariglio and Ruccio (2001) and Callari and Ruccio (1996). See also "The Genealogy of Postmodernism" by D. McCloskey (2001) in the afore-mentioned edited volume.
4. One of the hallmarks of the Enlightenment period and the concurrent emergence of modernity is that the search for True knowledge of the world through scientific inquiry was to replace the hallowed (though often erroneous) position of religion and ideology in attaining Truth:

> The men of the seventeenth century had seen words induce people to kill over the doctrine of transubstantiation, and they sought therefore a way to disarm words. Their refuge was 'crushing' proof and 'compelling' demonstration that which cannot possibly be doubted,

'putting Nature to the rack' as Bacon delicately put it (McCloskey, 2001, p.112).

5. Thus, not only are postmodern theorists skeptical of the promises made by metanarratives, they are altogether skeptical of the notion of a transcendent Truth. The postmodern position therefore, is characterized by a skepticism of the belief in science as a panacea to social evils.

6. Here postmodern theorists are standing on the shoulders of Kuhn, Feyerabend and Lakatos, who were among the first to be critical of the philosophy of science known as logical positivism" (or alternatively, the "Received View"). I discuss positivism and the literature critiquing it in the following pages of this chapter.

7. The work of Michel Foucault and Jacques Derrida were instrumental in disseminating the centrality of language and discourse in social theory. Foucault and Derrida brought to light how writing, texts and discourses bear on our construction and understanding of the natural and social worlds. "According to Foucault and Derrida, language and discourse are not transparent of neutral means for describing or analyzing the social and biological world. Rather they effectively construct, regulate and control social relations and institutions, and indeed, such analytic and exegetic practices as scholarship and research" (Luke, 1991). This "textual turn" in critical theory, known as Post-structuralism, unearthed the fact that institutionalized discourses such as Science, Medicine or Development, classify and regulate social spaces (such as the economy), practices (such as housework), people's bodies, identities and hence relations of knowledge and power.

8. Although I am arguing for the significance of local economic practices in the developing world, the work of Folbre (1993, 2001) as well as Fraad, Resnick and Wolff (1989) show that non-capitalist economic practices are rife even in advanced capitalist economies such as the United States. These authors point out the importance of household production in terms of both the number of people employed, as well as the value of their output. Yet, until brought to attention by feminist economists, the significance of non-market transactions of the household economy had been overlooked the in economic literature. Development literature has been aware of the fact that non-market transactions are just as much if not more significant in developing countries. As mentioned before however, these non-capitalist economic practices are seen as marginal to the (often smaller) capitalist sector.

9. The word teleology originates from the Greek word for end (telos) and perfect or complete (teleos). Critics point out that the narrative of economic development is teleological in that there is an underlying assumption that "progress through industrialization is the key to growth and the eradication of poverty and unemployment" (Chakrabarti and Cullenberg, 2003, p.3). In this evolutionary representation of societies, the advanced industrialized nations of the West have already arrived at this telos and to develop, "under" or "less" developed countries have to "catch up" to get to this preordained path. Chakrabarti and Cullenberg point out that the belief that

economies with predominantly capitalist activities are the telos for Third World societies is a particular understanding of the human condition. It is a view that is guilty of historicism—"a view that history has a pattern and a meaning that, if grasped, can be used to predict and fashion the future" (Bottomore, 1983 p.239). Karl Marx rejected historicism, arguing instead that "history itself had no meaning beyond that which men in their varying stages of development assigned to it" (ibid).

10. Capitalism, Gibson-Graham (1993) remind us, is the name for only one form of an economy.

11. Cullenberg (1999) notes, "how one conceives the relationship between the individual and society is the most fundamental decision of any social theory. The decision not only structures the manner in which theories apprehend the relationship between theory and the world (the epistemological issue) but also the ways in which the basic elements of a theory are causally related (the methodological issue)" (p.801).

12. Resnick and Wolff (1987) note that there is a clear hierarchy within the profession in which thinking about economic methodology is of secondary importance to "doing" economics: building models and testing their ability to explain and predict reality (Cullenberg et al., 2001). Nevertheless, this chapter hopes to persuade the reader that epistemological self-consciousness on the part of the theoretician and policymaker is crucial for development policymaking.

13. This belief that societies pass through progressively higher evolutionary forms has its origins in Hegelian philosophy. In The Philosophy of History, Hegel argues that human history can be understood as 'progress in the consciousness of freedom.' Human progress is achieved through the "world-spirit's" historical struggles for "a higher principle of freedom, a closer approximation of the truth, a higher degree of insight into the nature of freedom" (Bottomore, 1983, p.227). Progress, Hegel argues, directs human history towards Christianity, the reformation, the French Revolution and constitutional monarchy. For Hegel therefore, human history is meaningful and follows a predetermined pattern. Marx retains Hegel's belief that humanity makes progress in the course of history but argues that the subjects of history are restricted and that their actions are "determined by the material structure of the economic in the first or sometimes the last instance" (Chakrabarti and Cullenberg, 2003, p.13). Like Hegel, Marx also adopts a Eurocentric view of world history, as is apparent in his writings on India and China.

14. Descartes' is ubiquitously quoted for suggesting that it is by deductive reasoning or intuition that each man [sic] knows what he is. It was also Descartes in *Discourses on Method and the Meditation* (1968) "who stamped indelibly on modern thought the idea that the world was ultimately decomposable into a set of independently constituted parts and therefore that the proper method for understanding reality was to discover, and then analyze one by one its preexisting parts" (Cullenberg, 1999, p.803). His metaphor describing the relationship between the individual and society as a machine whose parts can be disassembled and examined separately continues to

dominate economics, as evident in the calls for establishing the microfoundations of macroeconomic theory.

15. David Hume noted that the human mind readily forms generalizations based on individual examples. Empiricists such as Mill and Hume viewed induction as a key process of scientific methodology. An inductive argument employs "premises containing information about some members of a class in order to support a generalization about a whole class" (Blaug, 1980, p.16). For example, the repeated observation of white swans over numerous independent occasions might lead the observer to conclude: "All swans are white." However, as Karl Popper pointed out, to make an inductive generalization based on a series of observations is invalid. The observation of a single black swan would invalidate the statement "All swans are white." Blaug (1980) mentions that the problem of induction originated with John Stuart Mill. Mills' *System of Logic*, Blaug remarks wryly, is a "eulogy to the logic of induction" (p.62). In advocating induction as a methodology of science, says Blaug, Mill failed to distinguish between discovery and proof. For an overview of rationalism and empiricism see Paul Edwards (1967), The Encyclopedia of Philosophy.

16. Early 20th century philosophers of science chose verifiability as the demarcation criterion for distinguishing a scientific statement from a non-scientific statement. A synthetic statement was considered to be cognitively meaningful if it were capable, in principle, of complete verification by observational evidence. Karl Popper (1983) however, noted that a certain type of statement, an affirmative existential statement, could be verified but not falsified. For instance, the statement "unicorns exist" could be verified by finding a unicorn but it could never be falsified, even if it is false. (Note that the failure to find a unicorn does not establish that none exist: they just haven't been found yet). Using the verificationist criterion however, "unicorns exist" would be a scientific statement. Popper's critique led to the adoption of falsification as the demarcation criterion, whereby, a hypothesis is scientific if and only if it is potentially falsifiable. Scientific progress therefore involved the critical examination and re-testing of hypotheses until the false theories were eliminated from the body of scientific knowledge. Falsified hypotheses, according to Popper, were more interesting because they lead to further testing and reexamination to see what went wrong. "Such critical reexamination offers best hope that false theories will be eliminated from science" (Caldwell, 1991, p.4).

17. For an economist's critique of Modernity see Arjo Klamer's *The Advent of Modernism* (unpublished manuscript).

18. Cullenberg (1999) points out that "the general equilibrium models in the tradition of Kenneth Arrow and Gerard Debreu are examples of an economy conceived of as a machine, where the economy (the totality) is understood as an equilibrium result of the interactions of pre-given agents (the parts).

19. Blaug cites Joseph Schumpeter for having coined the term "methodological individualism" and for distinguishing it from "political individualism." While methodological individualism refers to a theoretical practice in

economics, political individualism refers to "a political program in which the preservation of liberty is made the touchstone of government action" (1983, p.45).

20. Resnick and Wolff acknowledge that the term overdetermination "is borrowed from Freud, Lukács and Althusser and considerably modified by us" (1987, p.2). Callari and Ruccio suggest that by turning to psychoanalysis, Althusser exposed Marxism to a set of "well-developed concepts and modes of analysis" with which to theorize the "not yet existing, or that which does not yet exist as a conscious system, that which exists at the level of the 'imaginary'" (1996, p.39).

21. Feminist economists have also made significant contributions to the critique of the rationality assumption. See for example, England (1993) and Nelson (1993).

22. These two are not necessarily linked. Satisficing behavior for example, is also reductionist but not rational.

23. Colloquially this is exemplified in the well-known slogan "it's the economy, stupid." Mainstream economic theory is not the only guilty party in subscribing to economic determinism. Various Marxists including Althusser (see Cullenberg, 1999) have been criticized for believing in the economy as a determinant in the last instance. Neoclassical economists such as Becker (1991) have incurred the ire of social scientists (and economists) for reducing complex non-market, non-capitalist arenas such as the family, to the simplistic market logic of utility maximization.

24. For example, in their efforts to recognize the significance of non-market logic, Philip Mirowski (2001) and Stephen Gudeman (2001) look to the "gift" (the practice of prestation and counter-prestation) as a non-capitalist, culturally embedded social phenomenon that existed before capitalism and continues to exist alongside it.

25. This methodological imperative to "simplify, axiomatize, standardize, deculturalize, universalize" (2001, p.105) the social world McCloskey comments, is a characteristic of modernity.

26. Kenny and Williams (2001) show that econometric and theoretical models that have attempted to analyze growth have produced results that are contradictory.

27. In this instance the treatment of the historically voiceless peoples of the developing world can be likened to the treatment of the psychiatric patient as described by Foucault in Madness and Civilization (1965). In his essays on power/knowledge Foucault (1980) argues that there has been an "insurrection of the subjugated knowledges" of these voiceless people in the latter half of the 20th century. He argues in favor of this "insurrection" because they bring to light the hegemonic nature of "organized scientific discourse" (p.85).

28. For instance, contrary to conventional beliefs that population growth leads to increased poverty and worsening environmental degradation, RRA investigations, together with aerial surveys and questionnaires, revealed that in Kenya denser populations were associated with more, not fewer trees—a greater proportion of which were deliberately cultivated (Bradley

et al., 1985; Bradley, 1991). In Guinea, studies revealed that while the government's modern forest management techniques led to deforestation, the traditional, indigenous techniques had successfully protected forests for years (Fairhead et. al., 1992A).

29. Dogbe (1998) expresses this realization in a Ghanian proverb: "The one who rides that donkey does not know the ground is hot."

30. Goebel (1998) discusses the fact that "quick and dirty" participatory techniques are being integrated into the programming cycle of development projects to fulfill the "local participation" criterion of agencies, thus bypassing the more fundamental changes.

31. Sandra Harding (1993) uses this phrase to describe Neoclassical Theory's attempt to incorporate gender into economic analysis. She suggests that mainstream economics' response to feminist critiques of the androcentric bias in the discipline has been to simply add a gender variable to an econometric model's list of regressors.

NOTES TO CHAPTER THREE

1. Ikram (1980) argues that the 1952 Free Officers Revolution had no coherent economic policy and was more concerned with consolidating power than anything else. Even the redistribution of land in 1952 was motivated by the Free Officers' concerns for consolidating power rather than issues of equity. It wasn't until 1956 when the Suez Canal was nationalized that the State began to play a more active role in the economy. He suggests that the motive behind the nationalization of the Canal was to reduce foreign control rather than the public ownership of assets. Hansen (1975) suggests that the large-scale nationalization that took place beginning in the 1960s were based on the apparent failure of the private sector to set up large-scale industries, prompting Gamal Abdel Nasser to state: "We cannot leave the economy in the hands of the private sector" (Cited in Ikram, 1980).

2. Gamal Abdel Nasser was president from 1956–1973, Anwar el-Sadat from 1973–1980 and Hosni Mubarak has been president from 1981 to the present.

3. Springborg and Hansen have suggested that the Egyptian social contract has "de-politicized" the population by being "essentially a compact between ruler and urban population or even, more narrowly, between ruler and elite"(Hansen, p. 117), "the latter offering acquiescence and surrender of political rights in return for *la dolce vita*" (ibid, p. 250).

4. Khalid Ikram (1980) notes that "Pricing polices in Egypt were trying to achieve with deficient methods of price determination a variety of conflicting objectives. A single policy instrument cannot aim with success at the distribution of income, the allocation of resources, the control of aggregate demand, raising government revenues and so on."

5. While political dissidents have been arrested and imprisoned since the time of Gamal Abdel Nasser, rising incidents of violence against Western tourists and the tourism sector by Islamic fundamentalists are now punishable by death sentences (James Toth, 1999, p. 205).

6. Handoussa (1990) found that between 1978 and 1988, 75 percent of the authorized equity of total approved projects came from Egyptian nationals.

7. Egypt had signed a stabilization agreement with the IMF as early as 1962 when a failure in the cotton crop led to a foreign exchange crisis. However, relations with the Bretton Woods Institutions were estranged during the "socialist" era and it was not until Sadat's rapprochement with the US and the *Infitah* that Egypt signed a stand-by agreement with the IMF once again in 1977. This led to further agreements in 1979–81, 1987 and then finally the comprehensive structural adjustment programs in 1991 which will be discussed in the following section (See Abdel-Khalek, 2001 for detailed descriptions of the actual terms of these agreements).

8. The current figures are for 2001 from the Egypt Human Development Report 2003, table G.18.

9. Qena and Suhag are extremely close: Qena reports female (15+) literacy rates at 32%; Suhag reports 31.9%.

10. In rural Upper Egypt, the 2003 EHDR reports a female literacy rate of 20.3%.

11. Estimates of the number of Egyptians working abroad between 1974 and 1986 vary. A CAPMAS study carried out in 1987 estimated that about 1,964,000 were working abroad that year. Given that this was a year after the fall in oil prices, it would be safe to assume that at least two million Egyptians migrated to other Arab countries for work in the 1980s (see Richards (1994) for further discussion on this issue).

12. Using a relatively conservative poverty line, a 1990 World Bank study found that poverty fell from 44% of rural households in 1974/75 (1,833,000) to 24% or 1,023,000 households in 1981/82 (World Bank, 1990). Korayem (1987) used a higher poverty line and found that 29.7% of rural households (1,240,000) were in poverty in 1981/82.

13. "The South's greater emphasis on extended kinship relations" Toth remarks, meant literally a more clannish culture," (ibid, 207)). Moreover, he argues that among many *Sa'idis* the passage to modernity has been accompanied by a transition from the "passive quietism of Sufism" of rural Upper Egypt, to the "political activism of Salifiyism, legalism, and righteousness" (Gilsenan, quoted in Toth, 1999, p. 210).

14. The informal sector is difficult to define and enumerate by its very nature. In the development literature on Egypt it is generally understood as being outside the purview of government regulation.

15. The Ministry of Economy defines these as enterprises that employ between 1 and 14 workers (1998).

NOTES TO CHAPTER FOUR

1. Timothy Mitchell (2002, p. 182) provides a fascinating account of Luxor and Pharaonic Egypt's ambiguous place in the narrative of modernity and nation-building in Egypt. Although, anti-imperialism, pan-Arabism, and Islamism have dominated the ideological construction of the modern

Egyptian state, in its bid to build a cohesive national identity, the State has periodically used references to the militarism, leader-worship and imperialism of Ancient Egypt.

2. The State's Foucauldian "gaze" first fell on Luxor when Howard Carter discovered Tutankhamun's tomb in 1912. Mitchell (2002) documents that there have been ongoing attempts to plan and develop Qena and Luxor since 1945 and the area and its communities have been the "target population" of numerous development "missions." The most recent round of "planning Luxor" began in 1992; as an intern, I participated in the process in the year 2000.

3. Qena suffers from the dubious distinction of being the place that harbored the gunmen who attacked and killed four tourists in Luxor in 1992. In 1997, 60 people were killed in Luxor when gunmen fired on a tourist bus. The authorities claimed the attack was carried out by members of the *Gamaat-al-Islamiya*. The gravity of the situation for the State can be better understood if it is taken into consideration that tourism is the single largest foreign exchange earner in Egypt. The industry was hard hit by the event of September 11th in 2001 (http://www.ebusinessforum.com). In 2003, tourism revenues have risen back up to their pre-September 11th levels at US $4.3 billion. (http://www.amcham.org.eg/Publications/BusinessMonthlyDecember%2004/reports risingfuelcostscouldslowtourism).asp.)

4. A type of clover commonly used as fodder for cattle.

5. In 1999 Luxor's revenues accounted for about 10% of total tourism revenues for the country as a whole.

6. The government of Egypt's Ministry of Housing, Utilities and Urban Communities (MHUUC) and the United Nations Development Programme (UNDP) jointly sponsored the pre-planning and planning stages of the CDCL. Phase I involved environmental, geological and demographic assessments of the area. Phase II involved the actual development of a physical plan based on these surveys and was executed by an US consultancy firm (Abt Associates).

7. Representations of the local communities in relation to tourism is focused on their having a "negative impact," even though, Abu-Lughod points out, arguably it is tourism that contributes to the deterioration of the antiquities through "tourist buses that spew exhaust and tourists who breathe inside the tombs also cause serious damage to the monuments" (1999, p. 162).

8. As the major funding agency for the CDCL (along with the government of Egypt), this orientation placed the UNDP in a difficult position, especially given its official mandate of "Sustainable Livelihoods." The Sustainable Livelihoods Approach to development policy-making combines elements of human development, integrated rural development as well as participatory research. Based on a participatory assessment of the activities, entitlements and assets of communities, the Sustainable Livelihoods approach to policy-making proposes a methodology whereby *the local community identifies the various development projects it wishes to undertake*. The community representatives themselves then take the responsibility to undertake some of the work involved in the project using their own resources. Other aspects

of the work are undertaken by the local governments, civil society organizations, donors as well as the national government. The strength of the SL approach lies in co-coordinating the community indigenous strategies with policies at the local and national levels. The success of this co-ordination is dependent on the strengths and abilities of civil society organizations to convey the "voice" of the local communities to the higher echelons of policy-making circles.

9. Saskia Sassen notes that these special rights awarded to transnational firms on sovereign territory have disproportionately favored the owners of capital over workers. She points out that in these enclaves of capitalism nation-states have produced "new forms of legality" that allows concessions to transnational firms. These concessions have in effect "denationalized" national territory, a practice that has strengthened "the advantage of certain types of economic actors and weakens those of others" (Sassen, 1998, p. xxvii). While the privileges awarded to capital have been "imbued with positive values by many government elites and their economic advisors," she notes that concessions to workers tend to be imbued with negative values.

10. The thrust of the UNDP's intervention was based on the agency's mandate: to make development planning more "participatory" through processes operationalized in its "Sustainable Livelihoods" approach. This meant that not only should the CDCL's investment in infrastructure generate jobs for the local people, but also that they should be participants in the planning and implementation of the project itself. The challenge for the UNDP therefore was how to reconfigure a top-down, highly bureaucratic process into an interactive, participatory policy-making procedure.

11. The UNDP raised questions along the lines of "Does the local population possess the skills to work for the construction and tourism sector?" and "Are there vocational training schools in the area?" The agency's main intervention in the planning process was to find ways in which to "hook" up the local community to the CDCL's engine of growth—the tourism industry.

12. For instance, the British tourist company Thomas Cook has been operating in Upper Egypt and exporting tourist services since 1896.

13. The post-development literature has been critical of the notion of "planning" (see Marglin, 1990 and Escobar, 1992). The genealogy of planning, Escobar argues, can be traced back to the growth of urban cities in 19th century Europe, mobilizing industrial production during the First World War, Soviet planning, Taylorism and scientific management in the US and increased state intervention in the economy. Following the work of Michel Foucault, Escobar shows that the concept of planning embodies the belief that social change can be engineered and directed, produced at will. It is the idea that social change can be brought about in a way that leads to the better control and management of communities and their resources. Planning is propagated as being rational, objective, scientific, and about social and economic progress but it is often buttressed by ideology such as nationalism and often has significant material consequences for those involved.

14. The singular representation of "globalization" in the neoliberal literature is the equivalent of the singular and universal notion of "Modernity" (as I have discussed in Chapter I) where all modernities are judged by their approximation to Western Modernity and "Economic Development" (as I have discussed in Chapter II) where are all economies are judged by the degree to which they have converged to the western European or US capitalist system.

15. Although proponents of this outcomes centered view of globalization and development have argued, "Capitalism is a system that can destroy privilege and open up economic opportunity to many" (Bhagwati, 2002). Opponents of this view have argued just the opposite. Conceptualizing development as a homogenous set of outcomes such as capitalist economic growth has been exclusionary: benefiting some people while impoverishing others by excluding them from participating in global markets, from the economic policymaking that affect their daily lives, from the decision making processes that establish the conditions of their workplace and from partaking in the rising levels of income that have accompanied the distribution of global wealth (I spell out this argument in the Chapter One). Opponents of neoliberalism have instead argued for seeing development as a process rather than a set of outcomes (Cullenberg and Chakrabarti, 2003).

16. Based on these three moments of participation, Cullenberg (1992) categorizes labor practices by three degrees of exclusion: from independent class processes where workers who perform surplus labor are able to appropriate it in its entirety (and in that sense excludes all other members of society), to communal class processes where workers share the surplus labor they create, and lastly, to capitalist class processes where workers have no access to surplus labor.

17. Cullenberg argues that "a necessary but by no means sufficient condition for the 'good society'" is the "modest yet fundamental goal of collective appropriation" (1992, p. 7). He defines collective appropriation as a site "where there is democratic decision-making concerning the appropriation of surplus labor" (ibid, p. 23). The Mondragon cooperatives, which practice collective appropriation, exemplify an organizational form for an enterprise that is much more participatory than a capitalist enterprises.

18. That is to say, since each worker produces not only enough wealth to sustain him- or herself, but some amount beyond that, then each worker should also have a right to a share of that surplus. Cullenberg is clear about who should partake in the appropriation of surplus labor. He argues that this shared appropriation of surplus labor should be inclusive of all individuals employed at the initial site of surplus labor production (including that is, laborers, managers, clerical staff, etc) and that appropriation should be organized around "one person, one vote."

19. See Toth (1999, Chapter Three) for a detailed description and discussion on the gendered division of labor in Upper Egypt).

20. One of the frequently cited concerns in the literature on Egyptian agriculture is the incredible degree to which arable pots of land have been divided and then subdivided among family members through generations. Nevertheless,

until 1992, the trend in Egyptian agriculture had been moving towards reduced concentration in land ownership (Ireton, 1998). This trend had started as early as the 1930s, but had been accelerated by Nasser's Agrarian Reform law No. 178 in 1952. Legislation in 1952, then in 1961 and then again in 1969, placed ceilings on individual ownership of land to prevent land becoming concentrated in fewer and fewer landowners.

21. Patriarchy is defined as "a power system organized around male authority" (Grewal and Kaplan, 2002, p. 180). There is an extensive literature on the codependency of capitalist exploitation and patriarchal oppression (see for instance, Nash and Fernandez Kelly, 1983; Hartmann, 1976 and 1979).

22. Gibson-Graham and Ruccio also discuss a patriarchal communal class process (2001, p. 172). Resnick and Wolff provide a more detailed analysis of a patriarchal communal class process as one variety among three forms of communal class processes in *Class Theory and History: Capitalism and Communism in the USSR* (2002, pages 65–69).

23. There are two sugarcane factories in Luxor: one in Armant to the South and the other in Qus to the North. Two other factories are in Qena and there is one also in Aswan.

24. Sugarcane is not strictly distributed via the market mechanism in the sense that the crop is sold directly to state-owned sugar processing factories: the state subsidizes sugarcane production by buying from farmers at prices that are higher than those in the world market.

25. This section is based on conversations with Ahmed Ramsy (Senior Officer for the Social Fund for Development in Qena) as well as Amin Omar Mohammad (Administrative Officer, Ministry of Agriculture).

26. *Sugarcane in Egypt: Strategy for water management* (USAID Reform Design and Implementation Unit report # 33).

27. A 1993 World Bank study found that Egypt's comparative advantage calculated in terms of domestic resource costs lie in tomatoes, wheat and cotton and is least competitive in sugarcane and berseem.

28. Ostensibly, the CDCL's solution to the land constraint is to reclaim land from the desert. It does not however, discuss a) who will pay for the reclamation of land and b) how will land that is reclaimed be redistributed? Will the local community have access to this redistributed land given that the Government's land reclamation policy is geared towards relocating "new graduates" (meaning people with secondary school degrees) from the densely populated Delta regions? The existing reclaimed land policy offers "graduates" plots of 5 feddans and a loan of LE 25, 000 at an interest rate of 7%. They are to use LE 5, 000 as a down payment and the plot is to be paid for in installments over 30 years. Moreover, reclaimed land has little or no access to basic infrastructure such as water and electricity. Both are key inputs for Egyptian agriculture since the current system of irrigation involves having to lift the water about one to two meters from an irrigation canal into the fields. Traditionally farmers have lifted this water using the Archimedes screw, but now the most common way to irrigate is to use electric pumps rented from large farmers (those who own five feddans or more of land).

29. Mitchell's chapter "Heritage and Violence" in *Rule of Experts: Egypt, Techno-Politics, Modernity* provides an insightful analysis of the exclusionary tactics of the World Bank's development strategies.

30. The Bank has been involved with development planning in Luxor since the 1970s. These policy recommendations were based on a 1982 study survey of tourists carried out by the US management consultancy form, Arthur D. Little. The survey found that tourists complained of being badgered by local taxi drivers, peddlers and shopkeepers to buy something or hire their services. As a result of these findings, the firm recommended that the local government should issue no further peddlers' licenses.

31. Ikram (1980) notes that at that time 4,000 landlords owned the same amount of land as 2.6 million peasants.

32. This is similar to Serap Kayatekin's (2001) category of "cash-tenants" in Post-bellum Mississippi.

33. Historically renowned for its fertility, the soil of the Nile valley has become less fertile with the construction of the Aswan Dam. The Dam prevented the annual flooding of the Nile, which had maintained the fertility of the Nile valley. Since the construction of the Dam therefore, Egyptian farmers have had to increasingly resort to imported chemical fertilizer. The Dam has also led to increased water-logging.

34. Bush (1998) estimates that the number is close to 2 million, rising up to 14 million if families are taken into account. To get a sense of the proportion of people in agriculture who are affected, in 1998, there were about 4.9 million people engaged in agricultural work according to government statistics.

35. Cullenberg and Chakrabarti (2003) describe similar "faceliftment" measures that took place in the cities in India during the period of economic reforms and in the Narmada Valley when local communities were relocated due to the construction of a series of dams. They suggest that during such dispossession of a community's land, the State is forcibly appropriating not just their surplus labor, but their "shared environment":

> The cost of building the series of dams in the Narmada Valley project is simply not the displacement of the people from the well known conditions (such as land or property) that enabled them to reproduce their class activities but also the loss of the (shared) "environment" in which people have undertaken their various class processes . . . And in the end, when the process of dispossession from conditions of existence obliterates the shared environment, it is not the surplus but the entire shared environment that is appropriated (Chakrabarti and Cullenberg, p. 182).

36. There are times when the hidden transcript might "spring into view" (Scott, 1990). One instance of this occurred in 1996 when according to Mitchell, residents of Gurna threatened with eviction wrote a petition to the local government. In it they denied that they harm tourism or damage the safety of the monuments:

We do not understand who has fabricated these rumors. We come from the monuments and by the monuments we exist. Our livelihood is from tourism. We have no source of sustenance beyond God except for our work with tourism. . . . We are married to the tourists (Mitchell, 2002, p. 205).

NOTES TO CHAPTER FIVE

1. Similarly, Ardener (1995) found that ROSCAs exist among employees of the IMF in Bolivia.
2. The PBDAC is a state-managed bank that makes large long-term agricultural loans. Branches are located throughout Egypt and often constitute the only bank in a locality (Baydas, Bahloul and Adams, 1995).
3. The argument goes as follows: low savings level means that banks have less funds to loan out to businesses for investment, leading to lower capital accumulation, lower productivity and fewer workers being hired. How are savings to be mobilized? Through providing incentives to save by ensuring that the real rate of interest on deposits are positive, through providing an savings facilities (such as postal deposits in Japan) and through fostering a good savings ethic (Galal, 1996; Sachs, 1998).
4. Hoodfar (1999) found that even girls as young as eight participated in gam'iyas so they could buy sweets or stationary. Among her informants, installments carried from as little as 25 piasters to 100 Egyptian pounds. Singerman's study (1995) found sums of up to 1,000 pounds among wealthier people.
5. In his studies of local ROSCAs (arisan) in East Java Geertz notes that "Extended ties are of some importance, but the major unifying bonds are those of neighborhood, village and village cluster" (1962, page 244).
6. The studies I draw on in this chapter by Early (1998), Ghannam, (2002), Hoodfar (1999), Inhorn (1998) and Singerman (1995,1997) refer to both the old quarters of central Cairo as well as the newer neighborhoods of Giza. Singerman based her work on mostly ten contiguous neighborhoods. Hoodfar's areas of study were Bulaq Al-Dakrur and Umraniyah Gharbiyah (see map). Some of these neighborhoods date as far back as A.D. 969 and have been well known historically for their commercial significance—such as al-Darb al Ahmar, al-Gamaliyya, Bab al Shariyya and al Musky—for being the heart of the textile district.
7. Hoodfar, whose areas of study were Bulaq Al-Dakrur and Umraniyah Gharbiyah, compares the neighborhoods to shantytowns in Latin America.
8. There is also an alternative but similar word balad, where the noun al-balad refers to country, nation village or town. When something is described as al- baladi it is said to be distinctively Egyptian. Baladi can also have more of a rural connotation than sha'abi, which is associated with Cairo.
9. Having to come to know the monthly income of the households she studied, Singerman marvels that "Their skill and ability to save money is still, frankly, somewhat of a mystery. However, their success is partially due to

minimizing daily expenditures and shrewdly shopping for the best quality but least expensive food, clothes and other daily necessities (Singerman, page 156)." Similarly, the ability of low-income neighborhoods to generate considerable savings in the United States is documented by Perry (1987)

10. She also suggests that many people prefer the gam'iyas to escape state attention, regulation and taxation. This has less to do with the informal/illegal nature of these small savings pools and more to do with omnipresence of the Egyptian State. "Informal networks in Egypt serve the collective interests of excluded groups in an authoritarian political system that seeks to exclude men and women from formal political participation "(ibid.).

11. People who participate in gam'iyas do so out of an interest to improve the material conditions of their lives and the lives of their family, but they also participate in them to have access to one or more financial networks in their community. Their social, community-based nature gives people the "strength to save" (Gugerty, 2005, page 3). Or as Baydas, Bahloul and Adams note, "A surprisingly large number of people in Egypt—particularly women—put themselves in positions where they are forced to save (1995, page 659). In other words, a part of the popularity of gam'iyas can be attributed to simply maintain "a good credit rating" among the members of a community (whether it be in a workplace or neighborhood). By participating in ROSCAs, people establish a credit history among their community and in doing so they maintain their access to the communal reserve fund.

Bibliography

Abdel-Fadil, M. (1980). *The Political Economy of Nasserism: A study in Employment and Income Distribution Policies in Urban Egypt*, London: Cambridge University Press.

Abdel-Khalek, G. (2001). *Stabilization and Adjustment in Egypt: Reform or De-Industrialization?* Northhampton, MA: Edward Elgar.

Abu-Lughod, L. (1998). Television and the Virtues of Education: Upper Egyptian Encounters with State Culture. In Hopkins and Westergaard (Eds.) *Directions of Change in Rural Egypt*, Cairo: The American University in Cairo Press.

Adams, R. Jr. (1993). The Economic and Demographic Determinants of International Migration in Rural Egypt. *The Journal of Development Studies*, 30(1) 146–166.

———. (2000). Evaluating the Process of Development in Egypt: (1980–97 *International Journal of Middle East Studies*, 32, 255–275.

———. (2002) Nonfarm Income, Inequality and Poverty in Rural Egypt and Jordan. World Bank Working Paper.

Al-Ahram Weekly. Various Issues

Amariglio, J. (1988. The body, economic discourse, and power: An economist's introduction to Foucault. *History of Political Economy* 20: 583–613.

———. (1990). Economics as a Postmodern Discourse. In W. Samuels (Ed.) *Economics as Discourse*. Boston: Kluwer Academic Publishers.

Amariglio, J. and D. Ruccio, (1999). The Transgressive knowledge of 'ersatz' economics in R. Garnett Jr. (ed) *What do Economists Know? New Economics of Knowledge*. London and New York: Routledge,

Amin, G. (1995). *Egypt's Economic Predicament: A Study in the Interaction of External Pressure, Political Folly and Social Tension in Egypt, 1960–1990*. New York: Brill.

Aoki, M. (1987). The Japanese Firm in Transition in K. Yamamura and Y. Yasuba (Eds.), *The Political Economy of Japan*, Stanford: Stanford University Press.

Appadurai, A. (1991). Global Ethnoscapes: Notes and Queries for a transnational Anthropology in R. Fox (Ed.) *Recapturing Anthropology: Working in the Present*.

163

Apfel-Marglin, F. and S. Marglin, (1990)). *Dominating Knowledge: Development, Culture and Resistance.* Oxford: Clarendon Press.

Arestis, P and M. Marshall, (1995). *The Political Economy of Full-Employment.* Vermont: Edward Elgar.

Assad, R. (1997). The Employment Crisis in Egypt: Current trends and future prospects, *Research in Middle East Economics,* 2: 39–66.

———. (1999). The Transformation of the Egyptian Labor Market: (1988-(1998). Paper presented at the Economic Policy Initiative Consortium.

Assad, R and M Arntz. (2005). Constrained Geographical Mobility and Gendered Labor Market Outcomes Under Structural Adjustment: Evidence from Egypt. *World Development,* 33(3) 431–454.

Blackburn, J. and J. Holland, (1998). *Whose Voice? Participatory Research and Policy Change.* London: Intermediate Technology Publications.

Banuri, T. (1990)). Modernization and its Discontents: A Cultural Prespective on Theories of Development. In F. Apfel-Marglin, and S. Marglin, (Eds.) *Dominating Knowledge: Development, Culture and Resistance.* Oxford: Clarendon Press.

Baydas, Z. Bahloul and D. Adams, (1995). Informal Finance in Egypt: "banks" within Banks. *World Development* 23(4) 651–661.

Beneria and M. Roldan, (1987). *The Crossroads of Class and Gender: Industrial Homework, Subcontracting and Household Dynamics in Mexico City.* London and Chicago: University of Chicago Press.

Beneria, L and S. Feldman, (1992). *Unequal Burden: Economic Crisis, Persistent Poverty and Women's Work.* Boulder, CO: Westview Press.

Benhabib, S. (2004). *From Identity Politics to Social Feminism: A Plea for the Nineties.*

Best, S and D. Kellner, (1991). *Postmodern Theory: Critical Interrogations.* New York: Guilford Press.

Bhabba, H. (1984). Of Mimicry and Man: The Ambivalence of Colonial Discourse. *October,* 28:125–33.

Blaug. M, (1992). . *The Methodology of Economics Or How Economists Explain.* Cambridge: Cambridge University Press.

Bottomore, T. (1991). *A Dictionary of Marxist Thought.* MA: Blackwell Publishers.

Bouman, F. J. (1995). Rotating and Accumulating Savings and Credit Associations: A Development Perspective. *World Development,* (23)3 317–384.

Bowles, S and H. Gintis, (1976). *Schooling in Capitalist America: Educational Reform and Contradictions of Economic Life.* New York Basic Books, Inc, Publishers.

———. 1987. *Democracy and Capitalism: Property, Community, and the Contradictions of Modern Social Thought.* Basic Books, United States of America.

———. (2002). The Inheritance of Inequality, in the *Journal of Economic Perspectives,* 16 (3).

Bunch, R. (1985). *Two Ears of Corn: A guide to People-centred Agricultural Improvement,* World Neighbors, 5116 North Portland, Oaklahoma City, Oaklahoma 73112.

Bush, R. (1999). *Economic Crisis and the Politics of Reform in Egypt.* United Kingdom: Westview Press,.

Caldwell, B. (1991). Clarifying Popper, *Journal of Economic Literature.* Vol XXIX, March (1991).

Callari, A and D. Ruccio, (1996). *Postmodern Materialism and the Future of Marxist Theory: Essays in the Althusserian Tradition.* Wesleyan University Press, Hanover and London.

———. (1996). Introduction: Postmodern Materialism and the Future of Marxist Theory in A Callari and D. Ruccio, *Postmodern Materialism and the Future of Marxist Theory: Essays in the Althusserian Tradition.* Wesleyan University Press, Hanover and London.

Cameron, J. (2003). Feminizing the Economy: metaphors, strategies, politics, *Gender, Place and Culture.* 10(2).

Central Agency for Public Mobilization and Statistics (CAPMAS), (1999). *The Annual Statistical Yearbook.*

Cernea, M. (1985). *Putting People First: Sociological Variables in Rural Development.* New York: Oxford University Press.

Chakrabarti, A and S. Cullenberg, (2003). *Transition and Development in India.* New York: Routledge.

Chakraborty, D. (1997). The Time of History and the Times of Gods. In Lowe, L. and D. Lloyd, (Eds.), *The Politics of Culture in the Shadow of Capital.* Duke University Press, Durham and London.

Chambers, R, (1998). Afterword in Jeremy Holland and James Blackburn eds. *Whose Voice? Participatory Research and Policy Change.* London: Intermediate Technology Publications.

———. (1997). *Whose Reality Counts? Putting the first Last* London: Intermediate Technology Publications.

———. Participatory Rural Appraisal (PRA): Analysis of Experience, *World Development,* 22 (9) 1253–1268.

———. (1994). Participatory Rural Appraisal (PRA): Challenges, Potentials and Paradigm *World Development,* 22(10) 1437–1454.

Chang, H and I. Grabel, (2004). *Reclaiming Development: An Alternative Economic Policy Manual.* Zed Books, New York.

Clifford, J. On Ethnographic Allegory. In J. Clifford and G. Marcus (Eds.) *Writing Culture: The Poetics and Politics of Ethnography.* Berkeley: University of California Press.

Conway. G. (1985). Agrosystems Analysis, *Agricultural Administration* 20: 31–55.

———. (1986). Agrosystems Analysis for Research and Development Wintock International Institute for Agricultural Development, PO Box 1172, Nana Post Office, Bangkok, 10112.

———. (1987). Rapid Rural Appraisal and Agrosystems Analysis: A Case Study from Northern Pakistan, in KKU *Proceedings: 228–54.*

Cornwall, A. (2003). Whose Voices? Whose Choices? Reflections on Gender and participatory Development. *World Development,* 31(8) 1325–1342.

Crush, J. (1995). Imagining Development. In J. Crush (Ed.) *Power of Development,* Routledge Press London and New York.

Cullenberg, S. (1992). Socialism's Burden: Towards a Thin Definition of Socialism, *Rethinking Marxism*, 5 (2) 64–83.

———. (1998) Exploitation, Appropriation and Exclusion: Locating Capitalist Injustice in *Rethinking Marxism* 10(2).

———. (1999). Overdetermination, Totality, and Institutions: A genealogy of a Marxist Institutionalist Economics, *Journal of Economic Issues*, 33 (4) 1–15.

Cullenberg, S. J. Amariglio and D. Ruccio, (2001). *Postmodernism, Economics and Knowledge*, Routledge, London and New York.

Daly, G. (1991). The Discursive Construction of Economic Space: Logics of Organization and Disorganization. *Economy and Society* 20 (1).

Davidson, B. (1994). *The Search for Africa*. New York: Simon and Schuster.

Descartes, R. (1968). *Discourses on Method and the Meditation* Penguin Books, England.

Derrida, J. (1976). *Of Grammatology*. Johns Hopkins University Press, Baltimore.

De Soto, H. (2000). Dead Capital and the Poor in Egypt. *The Egyptian Center for Economic Studies*, Cairo.

Dogbe, T. (1998). The One Who Rides the Donkey Does not Know the Ground is Hot: CEDEP's involvement in the Ghana PPA. In J. Blackburn and J. Holland (Eds.) *Whose Voice? Participatory Research and Policy Change*. London: Intermediate Technology Publications.

Dow, S. (1991). Are there any signs of postmodernism in economics? *Method*, June 81–85.

Dow, S. (2001). Modernism and Postmodernism: A Dialectical Analysis. In Cullenberg, Amariglio and Ruccio (Eds.) *Postmodernsim, Economics and Knowledge*. Routledge Press.

Drèze, J and A. Sen, (2002). *India: Development and Participation*. Oxford University Press, New York.

Dymski, G and M. Floro. (2000). Financial Crisis, Gender, and {pwer: An Analytical Framework. *World Development* 28 (7).

Ehrenreich, B and A. Hoschilde (2002). *Global Woman: Nannies, Maids, and Sex Workers in the New Economy*. Henry Holt and Company, New York.

El-Laithy, H. M. Lokshin and A. Banerji, (2003). Poverty and Economic Growth in Egypt (1995-(2000). World Bank Policy Research Working 3068, June (2003).

Ellerman, D. Towards a Modern Theory of Property: A reconstruction Based on Old Ideas (draft).

El-Sadat, A. (1974). *The October Working Paper*. Cairo: Arab Republic of Egypt, Ministry of Information

Elyachar, J. (2002). Empowerment Money: The World Bank, NGOs and the Value of Culture in Egypt. *Public Culture* 14, (3).

England, P. (1993). The Separative Self: Androcentric Bias in Neoclassical Assumptions in Ferber and Nelson (eds.) *Beyond Economic Man: Feminist Theory and Economics*, The University of Chicago Press, Chicago.

Escobar, A. (1992). Planning. In W. Sachs (ed) *The Development Dictionary: A Guide to Knowledge as Power*. Zed Books, London, UK.

———. (1995). Imagining a Post-Development Era. In J. Crush (Ed.) *Power of Development*, London and New York: Routledge Press.

————. (1995). *Encountering Development: The Making and Unmaking of the Third World*. Princeton, New Jersey: Princeton University press.

Escobar, A and S. Alvarez, (1992). *The Making of social movements in Latin America: identity, strategy, and democracy*. Boulder, CO: Westview Press

Feyerabend, P. (1988). Knowledge and the Role of Theories, *Philosophy of Social Science*, 18, 157–78.

Ferguson, J. (1990). *The Anti-Politics Machine*. Cambridge University Press, Cambridge.

Fernandez-Kelly, P. (1997). For We Are Sold, I and My People: Women and Industry on Mexico's Frontier. Albany: State University of New York Press.

Folbre, N. (2001). *The Invisible Heart: Economics and Family Values*. New York: The New York Press.

Foucault, M. (1965). *Madness and Civilization*. Vintage Books, New York.

————. (1978). *The History of Sexuality*. Vintage Books, New York.

————. (1980). *Power/Knowledge: Selected Interviews and Other Writings*. The Harvester Press, Great Britain.

Frank, A. G. (1969. *Capitalism and Underdevelopment in Latin America*. New York: Monthly Review Press.

Freedman, R and James Medhoff. (1984) *What Do Unions Do?* New York.: Basic Books.

Freedman, R. (1993). Labor Market Institutions and Policies: Help or Hindrance to Economic Development? *Proceedings of the World Bank Annual Conference on Development Economics, (1992)*. The World Bank.

————. (1991)). Accountability in the Participatory Mode. *Canadian Journal of Development Studies*, xviii, special issue.

Fraad, H. S. Resnick and R. Wolff. (1994). *Bringing it All Back Home: Class, Gender and Power in the Modern Household*. Boulder, CO: Pluto Press.

Friedman, M., 1953. The Methodology of Positive Economics. In M. Friedman (Ed). *Essays in Positive Economics*. Chicago: University of Chicago Press.

Freire, P. (1968). *Pedagogy of the Oppressed*, New York: The Seabury Press.

Galal, A. (1996). Which Institutions Constrain Economic Growth in Egypt the Most? *Arab Economic Journal*, 6(Autumn).

————. Potential Winners and Losers from Business Formalization. http://www1.worldbank.org/devoutreach/article.asp?id=287

Galbraith, K. (1999). The Crisis of Globalization *Dissent*, 46,(3)

Garnett, R. Jr. (1999). *What Do Economists Know? New Economics of Knowledge*. London and New York: Routledge.

Geertz, C. (1962). The Rotating Credit Association: A Middle Rung in Development. *Economic Development and Cultural Change* 10(3) 241–263.

Ghannam, F. (1998). *Remaking the Modern: Space, Relocation, and the Politics of Identity in a Global Cairo*. University of California Press, Berkeley.

Gibson-Graham, J. K. (1993). Waiting for the Revolution, or How to Smash Capitalism while working at Home in Your Spare Time. In *The End of Capitalism as We Knew it: A Feminist Critique of Political Economy*. Cambridge, Massachusetts: Blackwell Publishers.

————. (1996). *The End of Capitalism as We Knew it: A Feminist Critique of Political Economy*. Cambridge, Massachusetts: Blackwell Publishers.

———. (2003). An Ethics of the Local. *Rethinking Marxism*, 15 (1).

———. (2004). Surplus Possibilities: Re-presenting Development and Post-development. Paper presented at the Conference on Economic Representations: Academic and Everyday, University of California, Riverside, April (2004).

Gibson-Graham, J. K. and S. Resnick and R. Wolff, (2000). *Class and Its Others*, University of Minnesota Press, Minneapolis.

Gibson-Graham, J. K. and Ruccio, D. (2001). After Development: Re-imagining Economy and Class. In Gibson-Graham, Resnick and Wolff (Eds.) *Re/Presenting Class: essays in Postmodern Marxism*. Durham and London: Duke University Press.

Gibson-Graham, J.K. (2006) *A Postcapitalist Politics*, University of Minnesota Press.

Goebel, A. (1998). Process, Perception and Power: Notes from 'Participatory' Research in a Zimbabwean Resettlement Area, *Development and Change*, 29(2).

Griffin, K. (1996). An Investment-led Strategy of Structural Adjustment in Sub-Saharan Africa. *Issues in Development*, Discussion Paper No. 16. International Labour Office, Geneva,

Griffin, K and M. Brenner, (2000). Domestic resource mobilization and enterprise development in Sub-Saharan Africa. Iin K. Griffin (Ed.) *Studies in Development and Systemic Transformation*. London, UK: Macmillan Press ltd.

Grosz, E. (1990). Philosophy. In S. Gunew (Ed.) *Feminist Knowledge: Critique and Construct*. Routledge, London.

Gudeman, S. (2001). Postmodern Gifts in S. Cullenberg, J. Amariglio and D. Ruccio (eds.), *Postmodernism, Economics and Knowledge*, Routledge, London and New York.

Gugerty, M. K. (2005). You Can't Save Alone: Commitment in Rotating and Savings Associations in Kenya.

Guha, R. (1989). *The Unquiet Woods: Ecological Change and Peasant resistance in the Himalaya*. Berkeley: University of California Press.

Guha, R. (1997). *Dominance without Hegemony: History and Power in Colonial India*. Harvard University Press, Cambridge, Massachusetts.

Gupta, A. (1998). *Postcolonial Developments: Agriculture in the Making of Modern India*. Duke University Press, Durham and London.

Haddad, L and A. Ahmed, (2003). Chronic and Transitory Poverty: Evidence from Egypt, (1997-(1999). *World Development* 31(1) 71–85.

Hall, S. (1992). The West and the Rest: Discourse and Power in *Formations of Modernity*, Stuart Hall and Bram Gieben (Eds.), Polity, Oxford.

Handoussa, H. (Ed.) (1997). *Economic Transition in the Middle East: Global Challenges and Adjustment Strategies*. Cairo, Egypt: The American University in Cairo Press.

Handoussa, H. and G. Potter (1991). *Employment and Structural Adjustment: Egypt in the (1990)'s*. Cairo, Egypt: The American University in Cairo Press.

Hansen, B. (1991). *The Political Economy of Poverty, Equity, and Growth: Egypt and Turkey, A World Bank Comparative Study*, Oxford University Press, Oxford.

Hansen, B amd S. Radwan, (1982). *Employment Opportunities and Equity in Egypt*. International Labour Office, Geneva.

Harding, S. (1986). *The Science Question in Economics*. Ithaca: NY: Cornell University.

Hartmann, H. (1981). The Family as the locus of Gender, Class and Political Struggle: the Example of Housework in *Theorizing Feminism: Parallel Trends in the Humanities and Social Sciences*, Hermann and Stewart (Eds.). Boulder, Colorado: Westview Press.

Harvey, D. (1989). *The Condition of Postmodernity*. Oxford: Blackwell.

Heiko, H and R. Stirrat. (2001). Participation as Spiritual Duty; Empowerment as Secular Subjection in B. Cooke and U. Kothari (Eds.) *Participation: the New Tyranny*. London: New York.

Hildyard, N. P Hegde, P Wolvecamp and S Reddy, (2001). Pluralism, Participation and Power: Joint Forest Management in India in B. Cooke and U. Kothari (Eds.) *Participation: the New Tyranny*. London: New York.

Himmelweit, S and Mohun, S. (1977). Domestic Labor and Capital. *Cambridge Journal of Economics* 1(1).

Hirschmann, A. O. (1958). *The Strategy of Economic Development*, New Haven: Yale University Press.

———. (1970). *Exit, Voice and Loyalty: Responses to Decline in Firms, Organizations and States*. Cambridge: Harvard University Press.

Hochschild, A. (1989). *The Second Shift*. New York: Viking.

Hopkins, N and K. Westergaard, (1998). *Directions of Change in Rural Egypt*. The American University in Cairo Press

Hoodfar, H. (1999). *Between Marriage and the Market: Intimate Politics and Survival in Cairo*. Cairo, Egypt: The American University in Cairo Press.

Hoksbergen, R. (1994). Postmodernism and Institutionalism: Toward a resolution of the Debate on Relativism *Journal of Economic Issues*, 28(3) 679–713.

Howitt, R. (1999). Indigenous rights and regional economies: rethinking the building blocks. Retrieved July 31, 2006 from http://www.communityeconomics.org/publications/howitt.html.

Ikram, K. (1980. *Egypt: Economic Management in a Period of Transition*. Baltimore: John Hopkins University Press.

Ireton, F. (1998). The Evolution of Agrarian Structures in Egypt: Regional Patterns of Change in Farm Size in Hopkins and Westergaard (Eds.) *Directions of Change in Rural Egypt*, Cairo: The American University in Cairo Press, Cairo, Egypt.

James, C. L. R. (1989. *The Black Jacobins: Toussaint L'Overture and the San Domingo Revolution*. New York: Vintage Books.

Jameson, F. (1991). *Postmodernism, or, the Cultural Logic of Late Capitalism*. Durham: Duke University Press.

Ironmonger, D,. (1996). Counting outputs, capital inputs and caring labor: estimating Gross Household Product. *Feminist Economics*, 2 (3): 37–64.

Kalecki, M. (1972. *Selected Essays on the Economic Growth of Socialist and Mixed Economies*. Cambridge: Cambridge University Press.

———. (1990). Political Aspects of Full Employment, in J. Osiatnyski (Ed.) *The Collected Works of Michal Kalecki*, Vol.1. Oxford: Oxford University Press.

Kenny, C. and D. Williams, (2001). What Do We Know About Economic Growth? Or, Why We Don't Know Very Much, *World Development* 29(1) 1–22.

Khedr, H. R. Ehrich and L. Fletcher, (1996). Nature, Rationale and Accomplishments of Agricultural policy Reforms, (1987-(1994 In L. Fletcher (Ed.) *Egypt's Agriculture in a Reform Era.* Ames, Iowa: Iowa State University Press.

Klein, N. (2000). *No Logo: Taking Aim at Brand Name Bullies.* New York.: Picador.

Knack, S and P. Keefer, (1997). Does Social Capital Have an Economic Payoff? A Cross Country Investigation. *The Quarterly Journal of Economics* 112(4) 1251–1288.

Korayem, K. (1996). Structural Adjustment, Stabilization Policies and the Poor in Egypt. *Cairo Papers in Social Sciences*, 18(4).

Kuczynski, P-P and J. Williamson, (2003). *After the Washington Consensus* Washington DC: Institute for International Economics.

Kuhn, T. (1962). *The Structure of Scientific Revolutions,* Chicago: The University of Chicago Press.

Laclau, E and C. Mouffe, (1985). *Hegemony and Socialist Strategy: Towards a Radical Democratic Politics.* Trans. W. Moore and P. Cammack. London: Verso.

Larter, C. (1997). Tourism has a bright future after a Boom year: Interview with Tourism Minister Mamdouh Al Beltagui. *Middle East Times*, January 18.

Longino, H. (1990). *Science as Knowledge: Values and objectivity in Scientific Inquiry.* Princeton, N. J.: Princeton University Press.

Lowe, L. and D. Lloyd, (1997). *The Politics of Culture in the Shadow of Capital.* Durham and London: Duke University Press.

Lyotard, J-F. (1984). *The Postmodern Condition: A Report on Knowledge.* Minneapolis: University of Minnesota Press.

Marglin, S. (1990). *Dominating Knowledge: Development, Culture and Resistance.* Clarendon Press, New York.

Marshall, M. (1995). Lessons from the Swedish Model in P Arestis and M. Marshall (Eds.) *The Political Economy of Full-Employment.* Vermont: Edward Elgar.

Marx, K. (1967). *Capital: a critique of political economy.* New York: International Publishers.

———. (1988). Economic and Philosophic Manuscripts of 1844. M. Milligan (trans). New York: Prometheus Books.

McCloskey, D. (1985). *The Rhetoric of Economics.* Wisconsin : University of Wisconsin Press.

———. (1994). *Knowledge and Persuasion in Economics.* Cambridge: Cambridge University Press.

———. (1999). Jack, David and Judith looking at me looking at them. in R. Garnett Jr. (Ed) *What do Economists Know? New Economics of Knowledge.* London and New York: Routledge.

———. (2001). The genealogy of postmodernism: An economist's guide in S. Cullenberg, J. Amariglio and D. Ruccio (eds.), *Postmodernism, Economics and Knowledge*, London and New York: Routledge Press.

Mirowski, P. (2001). Refusing the gift in S. Cullenberg, J. Amariglio and D. Ruccio (eds.), *Postmodernism, Economics and Knowledge*, London and New York: Routledge Press.

Mitchell, T. (1995). The Object of Development: America's Egypt In J. Crush (Ed.) *Power of Development*, London and New York: Routledge Press.

———. (2002). *Rule of Experts: Egypt, Techno-Politics, Modernity*, Berkeley and Los Angeles, California: The University of California Press.

Moser, C. (1998). The Asset Vulnerability Framework: Reassessing Urban poverty Reduction Strategies. *World Development*, 26(1) 1–19.

Muller-Mahn, D. (1998). Spaces of Poverty: The Geography of Social Change in Rural Egypt in Hopkins and Westergaard (eds.) *Directions of Change in Rural Egypt*, Cairo, Egypt: The American University in Cairo Press.

Nandy, A., 1983. *The Intimate Enemy: Loss and Recovery of Self under Colonialism*, New Delhi: Oxford University Press.

Narayan, D. R. Patel, K. Schaft, A. Rademacher and S. Koch-Schulte, (2000). *Voices of the Poor: Can Anyone Hear Us?* Oxford: Oxford University Press.

Nelson, J. (1993). The Study of Choice or the Study of Provisioning? Gender and Definition of Economics. In Ferber and Nelson (Eds.) *Beyond Economic Man: Feminist Theory and Economics*, Chicago: The University of Chicago Press.

North, D. (1990). *Institutions, Institutional Change and Economic Performance*, Cambridge: Cambridge University Press.

Ong, A. (1987. *Spirits of resistance and capitalist discipline: factory women in Malaysia* State University of New York Press, Albany.

Pollin, R and S. Luce, (1998). *The Living Wage: Building a Fair Economy*, New York: New Press.

Putnam, R. (1993). *Making Democracy Work: Civic Traditions in Modern Italy*. Princeton, NJ: Princeton University Press.

Putnam, R. (1995). Bowling alone: America's Declining Social Capital, *Journal of Democracy*, 1(6) pages 65–78.

Radwan, S. (1997). Towards Full Employment: Egypt into the 21st Century. The Egyptian Center for Economic Studies, Cairo.

Rahnema, M. (1992). . Participation In W. Sachs (Ed) *The Development Dictionary: A Guide to Knowledge as Power*. London, UK: Zed Books.

———. (1997). Introduction. In M. Rahnema and V. Bawtree (Eds.) *The Post-Development Reader*. Dhaka, Bangladesh: Zed Books.

Rahnema, M and V. Bawtree, (1997). *The Post-Development Reader*, Dhaka, Bangladesh: Zed Books.

Resnick, S and R Wolff, (1987. *Knowledge and Class: A Marxian Critique of Political Economy*, University of Chicago, Chicago and London.

———. ((2003). Exploitation, Consumption and the Uniqueness of US Capitalism. *Historical Materialism*, 11(4).

———. (2002). *Class Theory and History: Capitalism and Communism in the USSR*. Routledge, New York.

Rhoades, R. ((1982). *The Art of the Informal Agricultural Survey*, International Potato Center, Apartado 5969, Lima.

Richards, A. ((1994). The Egyptian Farm Labor Market Revisited *Journal of Development Economics*, 43(2).

Richards, P. (1985. *Indigenous Agricultural Revolution*, Hutchinson, London and Westview Press, Colorado.

Rodrik, D. (2003). *In search of prosperity: analytic narratives on economic growth*. Princeton,: Princeton University Press N.J.

————. (1997). Has Globalization gone too far? The Institute for International Economics: Washington, D.C.

Rostow, W. (1960. *The Stages of Economic Growth: A Non-Communist Manifesto.* Cambridge University Press.

Rostow, W. (1990). *Theorists of Economics Growth from David Hume to the Present: With a perspective on the Next Century.* New York: Oxford University Press.

Rowthorn, R and A. Glyn, (1990). The Diversity of the Unemployment Experience since (1973 in S. Marglin and J. Schor (Eds.) *The Golden Age of Capitalism,* Oxford: Clarendon Press.

Saad, R. (1999). State Landlord, Parliament and Peasant: The Story of the (1992). Tenancy Law in Egypt. In A. K. Bowman and E. Rogan (Eds.) *Agriculture in Egypt: from Pharaonic to Modern Times,* Oxford: Oxford University Press.

Sachs, J. (1996). Achieving Rapid growth: the road ahead for Egypt, *The Egyptian Center for Economic Studies,* Cairo.

Sachs, W. (1992). . *The Development Dictionary: A Guide to Knowledge as Power.* London, UK: Zed Books.

Said, E. (1979. *Orientalism,* New York: Random House.

Said, M. H. Chang and K. Sakr, (1997). Industrial Policy and the Role of the State in Egypt: The relevance of the East Asian Experience. In H. Handoussa (Ed.) *Economic Transition in the Middle East: Global Challenges and Adjustment Strategies.* Cairo, Egypt: The American University in Cairo Press.

Samuels, W. (ed) (1990). Economics as Discourse: An Analysis of the language of Economists. Boston: Kluwer Academic Publishers.

Samuels, W. J. (1991). Truth and discourse in the social construction of economic reality: an essay on the relation of knowledge to socioeconomic policy. *Journal of Post Keynesian Economics,* Summer 13(4) 511–497).

Sassen, S. (1998). *Globalization and Its Discontents.* New York: The New Press.

Scott, J. (1990). *Domination and the Arts of Resistance: Hidden Transcripts* New Haven, Connecticut: Yale University Press.

Screpanti, E. (2000). The Postmodern Crisis in Economics and the Revolution against Modernism, *Rethinking Marxism,* 12(1) 87–111.

Sen, A. (1999). *Development as Freedom.* Oxford: Oxford University Press.

Shiva, V. (1989. *Staying Alive: Women Ecology and Development,* London, UK: Zed Books.

Singerman, D. (1997). *Avenues of Participation: Family, Politics and Networks in Urban Quarters of Cairo.* Cairo, Egypt: The American University in Cairo Press.

Sen, A. (1981). *Poverty and Famines: An Essay on Entitlement and Deprivation,* Oxford: Clarendon Press.

————. (1999). *Development As Freedom.* New York: Alfred A. Knoff, Inc.

Shiva, V. (1992). Resources. In W. Sachs, (Ed.). *The Development Dictionary: A Guide to Knowledge as Power.* London, UK: Zed Books.

Soliman, S. (1998). State and Industrial Capitalism in Egypt. *Cairo Papers in Social Sciences* 21(2).

Springborg, R. (1989). Mubarak's Egypt: Fragmentation of the Political Order. Boulder, CO, and London: Westview Press.

Stiglitz, J. (1998). Towards a New Paradigm for Development: Strategies, Policies and Processes *Prebisch Lecture at UNCTAD.*

———. (2000). The Insider: What I learned at the World Economic Crisis. *New Republic,* 17(April).

———. (2000). Democratic Development as the Fruits of Labor. Keynote Address for the Industrial Relations Research Association, Boston.

Todaro, M. (1997). *Economic Development.* MA: Addison-Wesley.

Toth, J. (1999). *Rural Labor Movements in Egypt and Their Impact on the State (1961-(1992). .* Cairo, Egypt: The American University in Cairo Press.

Toulmin, S. (1990). *Cosmopolis.* New York: The Free Press.

United Nations Development Programme. *Human Development Reports,* various years.

———. *Egypt Human Development Report,* various years

Uphoff, N. (1992). *Learning from Gal Oya: Possibilities for Participatory Development and Post-Newtonian Social Science,* Ithaca and London: Cornell University Press.

USAID, (1999). Sugarcane in Egypt: Strategy for Water Management. USAID Reform Design and Implementation Unit, Report No. 33.

Vanek, J. (1979. Time Spent in Housework in N. Cott and E. Pleck, *A Heritage of Her Own: towards a new social history of American women,* pp. 499–506. New York: Simon and Schuster.

Wade, R. (2001). Showdown at the World Bank. *New Left Review,* January/February.

Wallerstein, I. (1974). *The Politics of the World Economy: The States, the Movements, and the Civilizations.* Academic Press, New York.

Watts, M. (1995). A New Deal in Emotions. In J. Crush (Ed.) *Power of Development,* London and New York: Routledge Press.

Williamson, O. (2000). The New Institutional Economics: Taking Stock, Looking Ahead, *Journal of Economic Literature,* 38(3) 595–613.

Wolff, R. 2006. Immigration and Class. Retrieved July 31, 2006 from http://www.rethinkingmarxism.org/.

World Bank, (1994). *Private Sector Development in Egypt: The Status and the Challenges.* A World Bank Report.

World Bank, (various years). The *World Development Report.* Oxford University Press.

Index

For Product Safety Concerns and Information please contact our
EU representative GPSR@taylorandfrancis.com Taylor & Francis
Verlag GmbH, Kaufingerstraße 24, 80331 München, Germany